1/17 9K

101
ESSENTIAL
CHINESE
MOVIES

SIMON FOWLER

101 Essential Chinese Movies
Copyright © 2010 Simon Fowler

ISBN-13: 978-988-19091-1-4

China Economic Review Publishing (HK) Ltd publishing for Earnshaw Books, Hong Kong

For Jem. This is really all your fault.

CONTENTS

Acknowledgements

Thanks be to Graham Earnshaw for soapy sashimi but mainly for saying "yes". Derek Sandhaus for editing my words into a state fit to print (his Zen-like patience should also not go unacknowledged). Gissing Liu and Chunzi Wang go together for constantly making my list longer (and better) and for finding the nuggets of information that were out of my reach. Serene Zhang for her last-minute photo help. Eveline Chao was there at the beginning, pointing me in the right direction and for that I'm eternally grateful, as I am to Julian Fisher, Matthew Plowright and Steve Webb for giving me all the encouragement I could ever need. How could I not thank Ben Shaw when he's the reason I'm in China? My family (Mum, Dad, Jem, Sis, Dave, Nick, Jules, Buddy, Rosie and Arthur) get thanked as one, but their significance permeates everything within this book (and everything outside of it, too). The good people at *Time Out Beijing* (especially Adrian Sandiford) for putting up with me, and giving me a sympathetic ear and a shoulder to cry on, and, last but by no means least, I'd like to thank Ruth Woodrow for being with me every single step of the way.

Introduction

Why on earth not include any films from Hong Kong or Taiwan? This is the most common question people asked me while I was writing this book. The reason is simply that so much has already been written about them. Chances are that when most people think about "Chinese" cinema, they imagine Bruce Lee and Jackie Chan. With this book, I wanted to look at something different, to look at the Mainland and the way its cinema has developed over the last century.

I started out as a film fanatic who just happened to be in China, but over time I inevitably made the transition into a Chinese film fanatic. Before arriving in China, my exposure to Chinese films was limited to art house fare that had excited European distributors enough to make it into the UK. I'd seen *Farewell My Concubine* and the later films of Zhang Yimou, but what I lacked most was the context in which to understand these films.

From the moment I arrived in Beijing, I became aware of a drastic difference between the Chinese films that are popular in China and those that are popular abroad. My Chinese friends, for instance, sang the praises of the film *Crazy Stone*, a comedy which baffled me when I first watched it, although its energy was infectious. The more I watched and read about Chinese films, the more convinced I became that a general overview of key Mainland movies would be a great starting point for people looking to learn more about the country's history and culture. And that's how this project was born.

I began at the beginning and discovered my first alarming fact about Mainland Chinese movies. Although China be-

FOUNDING OF A REPUBLIC (2009)

gan producing its own films in 1905 with *The Battle of Ding-junshan*, not a single film from before 1922 remains intact today. The nitrate film stock, which was used by pioneers of cinema around the world, is one of the most volatile materials you could imagine. Highly flammable, it had to be kept dry and safely stored otherwise it would become damaged beyond repair. This 17-year period of "darkness" has robbed us of several classic films, about which we now have only secondary information. *The King of Comedy Visits Shanghai* – made by the same production company as the earliest film in this collection, *Cheng the Fruit Seller* – was a fictionalized account of the visit of Charlie Chaplin (never named as such) to Shanghai. This blatant homage indicates the power and influence that Hollywood had on early Chinese cinema, but sadly the film is now lost. *The Burning of the Red Lotus Temple* took some pointers from US cinema, but was an entirely Chinese construction. Kung fu films inspired by *wuxia* (martial arts) novels and acrobatic performances flooded the Chi-

SONS AND DAUGHTERS OF THE GRASSLAND (1974)

nese market in the 1920s, and *The Burning of the Red Lotus Temple* spawned many sequels and knock offs. We can only speculate what this hugely popular film was like by viewing its imitators, like *Red Heroine*. The loss of these films was the first great tragedy in China's cinematic history, but it wasn't the last.

China was slower than many nations to wake up to the "talkie" revolution, but the 1930s are still often considered to be the "Golden era" of Chinese cinema. Silent films like *Little Toys*, *The Goddess* and *Street Angel* – starring glamorous actresses like Ruan Lingyu and Zhou Xuan – extolled the exotic beauty of Shanghai (and its women). Whereas pioneers of film in other countries like DW Griffith (America) and Yasujiro Ozu (Japan) were uneducated men, filmmakers in China were mostly leftist intellectuals who used their films to promote anti-Japanese, pro-labor sentiments.

Watching these films gave me my first understanding of how the fate of China's film industry was (and to an extent

4

still is) inextricably linked with its political fortunes. Politically and economically, Shanghai in those years was an island, with greater freedoms than in those areas controlled by the Japanese forces that had occupied most of coastal China by the late 1930s. The output from studios like Mingxing helped to rally the Chinese people against the invaders. Most of the films ended on a somber note, usually with a death occurring in the final act. It's almost as if the audiences in those days demanded an unromanticized take on events that would reflect the bleakness of their own lives. Filmmakers also ventured into new genres during this period, many of which never had the chance to catch on, with animation features like *Princess Iron Fan* and horror movies like *Song at Midnight*.

The arrival of Chairman Mao on the political landscape and the forming of the People's Republic of China in 1949 had a dramatic impact on China's film industry. Within a year, all independent film companies were nationalized, and much of China's key filmmaking talent left Shanghai for Hong Kong.

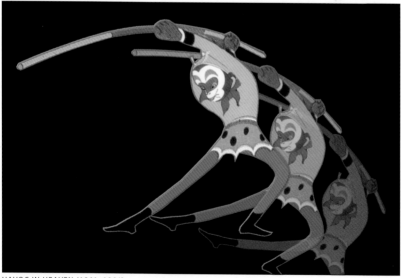

HAVOC IN HEAVEN (1961; 1964)

5

STILL LIFE (2006)

Mao understood the power of film as a propaganda tool, and consequently the number of cinemas in China quickly grew from 646 in 1949 to 20,363 in 1965. But the content of the films had to change, and plot diversity was the first casualty of the new era. At first, the majority of films were set in the not too distant past and usually featured some kind of evil landlord to remind everyone just how terrible things had been before the communists turned up. The endings of films changed, too, because there was no situation so bleak that it couldn't be resolved with the *deus ex machina* of the arrival of the People's Liberation Army, as in the films *An Orphan on the Streets* and *This Life of Mine*.

Of the films from the 1950s, one always stands out in my mind. Xie Jin's *Woman Basketball Player No. 5* was the first Chinese film I saw that was directed with urgency, flair and great technical ability. The bright colors, fast-paced sports scenes and sincere tone impressed me greatly. Of the many common threads that can be traced through the entries of this book, Xie's story is perhaps the most interesting. His life and career reflected the fortunes of China's film industry from the 1950s to 1970s, and his output was consistently of a high standard. It's perhaps most telling that he suffered more than others when the second disaster of China's movie industry struck in 1966.

The Cultural Revolution (1966-76) was a period of great upheaval. For ten years, film production practically ground to a halt. Mao's wife Jiang Qing (herself once an actress – see *Blood on Wolf Mountain*) oversaw the production of "model operas" like *Sons and Daughters of Grassland*, but most of the major players in the film industry found themselves persecuted for "bourgeois tendencies". And so, just as the People's Republic of China's film industry was finding its stride, its infrastructure was set back many years.

One entry in this book is a complete cheat based on my criteria for inclusion: *Chung Kuo – Cina*. The documentary was

THE SWORDSMAN IN DOUBLE-FLAG TOWN (1991)

made by Italian director Michelangelo Antonioni, but it was shot in China during the Cultural Revolution at the behest of Mao. It is included here because it gives cultural and political insight into this largely opaque era. It also provides a context for the filmmaking phenomena that would follow soon after its release.

With the death of Mao in 1976 and the opening up of China soon thereafter, a flood of films were made that railed against the political persecution of the past decade. So called "scar" films, which explored the circumstances behind the Cultural Revolution, became highly popular. Director Xie Jin created some of the most important works in this genre, like *The Legend of Tianyun Mountain*.

As Xie and his fellow directors began to pick up from where they had left off ten years before, an important institution was reopened: the Beijing Film Academy. Among the school's historic first batch of graduates were many of China's most widely heralded directors of all time. Chen Kaige, Zhang

8

Yimou and Tian Zhuangzhuang, among others, became known as the "Fifth Generation" of Chinese filmmakers. They exploded onto the scene, producing radical films that went against everything that had come before them. *Yellow Earth*, *One and Eight*, *The Horse Thief* and other films of the era captured the world's attention, putting China on the cinematic map.

Modern filmmaking in China began with these films. Just as the nation's economy began to adapt and mature, so did its movies. The Fifth Generation, as rebellious as the decade that spawned them, soon mellowed and began to move into the mainstream. It was this adoption of conventional styles that annoyed the next generation of filmmakers that popped up in the 1990s, called (you've guessed it) the Sixth Generation. Jia Zhangke, one such director, is the most widely known contemporary Chinese filmmaker in the West, but his introspective and thoughtful works like *Still Life* are rarely seen in China. Stop someone on the streets of Shanghai and

THE GODDESS (1934)

ask them who their favorite director is, and they'll probably say Ning Hao (*Crazy Stone*) or Feng Xiaogang (*A World Without Thieves*). These two have managed to capture the popular imagination of Chinese people, commenting on their foibles but also presenting a more positive view of society that reflects the optimism of the moment. With this book, I've tried to capture a sense of both these trends: you'll find plenty of Jia Zhangke and Zhang Yimou, but there are also a number of films that will appeal more to Chinese viewers than they ever will to foreigners.

I have sped through over a hundred years of cinematic history pretty quickly in this book, but I hope you will find some insight into this complex and fascinating industry and art form. With every entry you read, you'll find references to a number of other films that could easily have made it into the collection (and I encourage you to do your own digging for titles that have slipped through the net). This book could very easily have contained 250 titles, but rather than getting lost in an overly detailed survey of the Chinese cinematic terrain, I wanted to highlight the key points and places, to show you the best (or at least most notorious) examples of a particular kind of cinema. As you read about a film you might be interested in watching, you'll be glad to know that there are many more like them out there. So read and then watch.

Simon Fowler
Beijing, October 2010

FOREVER ENTHRALLED (2008)

11

Ershisi Chengji

24 City
2008

Jia Zhangke's work often has the air of a documentary. The natural performances he elicits from his actors, coupled with a slow, methodical cinematic style, encapsulate the day-to-day realities of life in urban China. His film *24 City* takes this pursuit of authenticity a step further. The film is based upon a true story and many of the "actors" are actually playing themselves, delivering monologues adapted from real interviews. If you're not aware of which actors are the professionals, you might not be able to distinguish the film's fiction from its reality.

The story (much like that of Jia's *Still Life*) focuses on the man-made destruction of communities on a massive scale. In 2006, an aviation factory in Chengdu – housing 30,000 workers and 100,000 of their family members – was slated for demolition to make way for a new apartment complex called "24 City". Hearing the story, Jia placed an ad in a local newspaper and interviewed over a hundred of the factory workers. What started as a mission to record the oral history of a fast-disappearing world soon grew into something more complex. The interviews explained much about these people's lives, but there was still something missing. Jia decided to bring in some well-known actors – including Joan Chen (*Lust, Caution*) and Zhao Tao (star of Jia's *The World*) – to produce a series of monologues that he could intercut with the real-life interviews to create, in his own words, a "panorama".

Jia is obsessed with exploring the effects of China's surge to economic supremacy, and the persistence of memory is

Director
Jia Zhangke

Screenwriters
Jia Zhangke
Zhai Yongming

Cast
Joan Chen
Chen Jianbin
Zhao Tao

Running time
112 minutes

a key factor in this film. When the buildings that symbolize the lives of over 100,000 people and their relationships are destroyed, what is left in its place? High-resolution digital video adds another layer to the film's grittiness. The surroundings are presented as they actually are, with no cinematic embroidery to separate us from the reality of what we see. Jia's images fascinate us and his story grips us with its frankness and the plausibility of its circumstances.

And the Spring Comes
2007

Lichun

Director
Gu Changwei

Screenwriter
Li Qiang

Cast
Wu Guohua
Jiao Gang

Running time
105 minutes

Individuality is neither easily cultivated nor tolerated in China. Whereas in the West a certain amount of quirkiness is found endearing, it's greeted mostly with suspicion in a population raised on the tenets of collectivism. Gu Changwei is attracted to stories (like that in his debut film, *Peacock*) about individuals who don't fit into China's rigid society. In his second film, *And the Spring Comes*, Jiang Wenli (Gu's wife) stars as Wang Cailing, a woman who aspires to become an opera singer to escape her mundane small-town existence. She works as a vocal coach at the local school, but her talent for singing Western opera is overshadowed by an unfortunate skin condition. Yet she still dreams of one day performing at the national theater.

Wang comes into contact with kindred spirits, all predictably quirky. Zhong Yu (Wu Guohua) and his friend Huang Sibao (Li Guangjie) take notice of Wang when she lies about having "connections" in Beijing. Huang is a frustrated artist, who hopes he can use Wang to get into the Beijing Art Academy. He leads her on, only to spurn her advances on a disastrous trip to Beijing. Zhong, meanwhile, really has fallen for the silver-voiced singer. Also in the group is Hu (Jiao Gang), an effeminate ballet dancer hell-bent on angering the locals. Nothing seems to go right for the group, which is heckled at a public performance. In chasing her dreams, Gu travels down a humiliating path, and it's only when she accepts that her best option may be her teaching career that she finds solace.

Striking a sympathetic chord, Gu's film is a light-hearted look at those who are desperate to rise above mediocrity, but somehow find themselves drowning in it. Jiang Wenli's performance was widely praised in the international film circuit, and it would take quite a heartless soul not to pity the downtrodden character she portrays. The setting is also a masterstroke. The harsh reality of Beijing's ugly urban skyline brilliantly contrasts with the lofty aspirations of the characters, who would do anything to escape their respective existences, but just don't have the skills to do it.

Ji Jie Hao

Assembly
2007

Listening to horns playing a melancholic dirge throughout the opening credits, we become aware that *Assembly* is a different kind of Chinese war movie – more reflective than triumphant. Made in 2003, we know that the action and plot were not constructed *entirely* to serve a political end – no Japanese "devils" here, just a realistic depiction of the war between the Communists and the Nationalists. In the competent hands of director Feng Xiaogang, whose barnstorming action is unlike anything seen in Chinese cinema before, the film draws easy (but unfair) comparisons with Steven Spielberg's *Saving Private Ryan*.

The film opens in the midst of a chaotic urban conflict in snow-drenched northeast China. Captain Gu Zidi (Zhang Hanyu) leads the People's Liberation Army Ninth Company in an attack against the KMT. Despite his victory, Gu is so enraged by the death of his political officer that he shoots KMT soldiers in cold blood. After serving a short sentence, Gu is plucked from the slammer to lead the Ninth Company in what amounts to a suicide mission to defend a vital coal mine from KMT forces. He is told to hold his position until the bugle of retreat is sounded, but over the course of the bloody action, his hearing is impaired and he is unable to decipher the signal. Outnumbered and outgunned, they fight until he is the last man standing. The first hour of the film features action shot in high-saturation akin to *Saving Private Ryan*, but the action gives way to a more dramatic second half. Two months after the battle, Gu – now in a war hospital – is unable to prove who he is. Several years later,

Director
Feng Xiaogang

Screenwriter
Liu Heng

Cast
Zhang Hanyu
Deng Chao
Yuan Wenkang
Tang Yan
Wang Baoqiang
Liao Fan
Hu Jun
Ren Quan
Li Naiwen

Running time
124 minutes

16

he moves to the Korean Peninsula to fight against the South Koreans and Americans, meanwhile saving the life of Er Dou (Deng Chao), an old war buddy. The remainder of the film deals with Gu's personal mission to regain the honor of his company, which has been all but forgotten in the annals of history.

This compelling film is all the more powerful because it is based upon a true story. Combining tender moments with horrific, stylized bloodshed, it was one of the highest-grossing films of 2007. Proving his versatility once again, Feng Xiaogang's decision to abandon the comedic genre, in which he is more comfortable, and attempt a gritty war drama was admirable; and it was even more admirable that he created a Chinese war film that doesn't (overtly) bang its chest in patriotic fervor.

Ren Dao Zhongnian

At the Middle Age
1982

The 1980s marked the beginning of the end for films like *At Middle Age*. Chinese realism as a genre would remain popular, but the explosion of exciting new styles on the screen meant that these more thoughtful, gentle films lost their relevance. But in its understated approach, *At Middle Age* tells us much about Chinese society.

The Chinese people know a thing or two about societal pressure. The Communists necessitated conformity, as did the Confucians before them. Lu Wenting (played with elegant beauty by Pan Hong) is a middle-aged doctor, struggling with the difficulty of balancing her work, family and personal life. She suffers a stress-related heart attack and finds herself in critical condition. The emaciated, pale figure lying on a hospital bed is hardly recognizable as the bright-eyed doctor who first took up her position 18 years earlier; a change that deeply saddens the department director. Lu's spirit has been ground down because of the mistreatment of doctors in Chinese society. Doctors and other intellectuals had been maliciously portrayed in movies and treated even worse in society. During Lu's convalescence she laments her inability to be a good mother or a good doctor with the mounting pressures of hard work and family life.

One day, an old college friend, Jiang Yafen, comes to visit her. Jiang, similarly disillusioned, has decided to emigrate to another country, where she and her husband believe doctors are better respected. Jiang cannot fully move on, however. As she boards the plane, she looks back with a

Directors
Wang Qimin
Sun Yu

Screenwriter
Shen Rong

Cast
Pan Hong
Zhao Kui
Da Shichang
Pu Ke
Zheng Qianlong

Running time
83 minutes

yearning for her motherland. In a letter, she promises Lu she will one day return.

After extended periods of rest and recovery – relying on her doting husband, the polite hospital staff and the indomitable spirit of her son – Lu eventually walks out of the hospital and returns home for the final stage of her recovery.

The sensitivity with which the story is told will not suit everyone's tastes, but Wang Qimin and Sun Yu's film unfolds at a sedate but pleasurable pace. It conveys its message with subtlety and clarity. This approach is greatly enhanced by the film's emotionally restrained score, somewhat reminiscent of that in Arthur Hiller's *Love Story*, which plays throughout. Its sweeping strings add a layer of gloom to the work, accentuating and informing the emotional peaks and troughs.

Bei Kao Bei, Lian Dui Lian

Back to Back, Face to Face
1994

Huang Jianxin is one of the greatest satirists in China, a country that isn't big on irony. He often hits painfully close to home by exposing the farcical situations caused by many of China's cultural tendencies. His films, however, don't just poke fun without reason, but rather criticize unfairness and double standards in contemporary Chinese society.

In *Back to Back, Face to Face*, an ancient city's provincial cultural office is used as a microcosm for the political processes of Communist China. The deputy director, Li Shuangli, is a competent man, constantly overlooked for promotion despite successfully running his office for years. When the position comes up, Li takes the unprecedented step of nominating himself, an act criticized by other senior staff members as "selfish". The job eventually goes to Ma, a bumpkin wheeled in from the countryside. Sensing the opportunity to exploit Ma's naivety, Li sets up a construction project that financially benefits the office employees. Li's strange attempts to manipulate Ma eventually lead the latter to tender his resignation, leaving open the much-desired position. Although Li is still the best candidate, the position goes to a buddy of one of the senior officials who exploits his *guanxi* (connections) to get the job. Yan is a bit of a thug and when Li's father accidentally damages Yan's new leather shoes, the money is deducted from Li's salary. The situation literally makes Li sick and, realizing his political attempts are getting him nowhere, he loses interest in office affairs. He turns his attention instead to applying for a permit to have another child (the one-child policy has left him with

Directors
Huang Jianxin
Yang Yazhou

Screenwriters
Huang Xin
Sun Yi'an

Cast
Niu Zhenhua
Lei Luosheng
Li Qiang

Running time
138 minutes

20

a daughter when he wanted a son). His wish is granted and his wife becomes pregnant. Once again, opportunity knocks when Director Yan is framed for watching porn and fired. By now, however, all Li cares about is his family and he no longer has an interest in the promotion, even if it were to be offered to him.

The social criticism in this film is subtle, but biting. The double-dealing and thirst for power so common in contemporary Chinese life is used to emphasize a growing shift away from socialist ideas and back towards the traditional family values they had supposedly replaced. The film's biggest irony, though, came years after its release. In 2009, Huang Jianxin – after making so many films critical of the Chinese government – was hired co-direct *The Founding of a Republic*, quite possibly the most chest-beating, jingoistic pro-Communist film ever made. It seems Huang really *does* understand his Chinese politics.

巴尔扎克 与小裁缝

Ba'erzhake yu Xiao Caifeng

Balzac and the Little Chinese Seamstress
2002

Balzac and the Little Chinese Seamstress is not the only Chinese film of the naughties made with a Gallic feel. As Chinese directors – who have been festival darlings since the early 1980s – count on discerning European cinemagoers to provide the bulk of their international box office sales, it was only a matter of time before French companies started to provide financing for their films. Director Dai Sijie, who had left China for France on a scholarship in 1984, was an early recipient of such support. He directed three successful films (two of them China-focused) before adapting his own semi-autobiographical novel, *Balzac and the Little Chinese Seamstress*, in 2004. The book was originally published in French, but the film's dialogue is almost entirely in Sichuanese. This was just one of many changes Dai made in adapting his book, because he recognized that a novel must often be reworked to achieve the same success on screen.

Ma (Ye Liu) and Luo (Kun Chen), like many young urbanites during the Cultural Revolution, are sent to the countryside to work the land and to be "re-educated". As both are the children of disgraced intellectuals, they are given a stern grilling about their "reactionary backgrounds" by the village chief upon their arrival. The boys are assigned to menial labor, helping the villagers in the local mine. Fate deals them a gift in the form of a young girl from a neighboring village, known as the Little Seamstress. Instantly infatuated, the boys are eager to win her affections and, despite her illiteracy, help in her education. The pair read to her from a stash of contraband Western books, including

Director
Dai Sijie

Screenwriters
Dai Sijie
Nadine Perront

Cast
Zhou Xun
Liu Ye
Chen Kun
Wang Hongwei

Running time
111 minutes

the works of Dostoevsky and Kipling. But her favorite writer is Balzac. Ultimately, the Little Seamstress chooses Luo and becomes pregnant with his child. Ma helps her to have an abortion – without Luo's knowledge – and life continues as before. One day, the Seamstress (excited by the new ideas she's learned) takes off for the city in search of a new life despite Luo's protestations. The film picks up again in the early '90s. Ma has become a violinist in France and Luo a professor at a dental institute in Shanghai, but neither have any idea what happened to the Seamstress. When they hear that the Three Gorges Dam will totally submerge the village they had stayed in, they journey back to find what's left of the town.

Although sometimes veering a little too close to *Dead Poets Society* in championing the universal power of literature, *Balzac and the Little Chinese Seamstress* remains a beautifully shot and cleverly crafted film. Zhou Xun is captivating in her performance as the Seamstress, enlivening this subtle tribute to a lost generation of China's youth.

The Banquet
2006

Ye Yan

Hamlet does not obviously lend itself to the historical kung fu genre, but no matter what he does director Feng Xiaogang seems to have a golden touch with Chinese audiences. His Shakespearean adaptation, *The Banquet*, was far more successful than its detractors would have you believe. The film features a star-studded cast including Feng-favorite Ge You – an actor with tremendous depth and subtlety – as well as Zhang Ziyi and Zhou Xun, currently two of China's most accomplished young actresses.

Crown Prince Wu Luan (Daniel Wu) is the Chinese answer to Shakespeare's melancholy Dane. He is in love with Little Wan (Zhang Ziyi), but his father is also keen on her, and takes her as his wife. Distraught, Wu Luan retreats into the countryside and only returns when he hears that his father is dead. It quickly becomes clear that the emperor was murdered by his brother, who has since been crowned as Emperor Li (Ge You). To add more salt to the wound, Li has taken Wan as his empress. Following many of the same dramatic turns as *Hamlet* – including a staged play to expose the murderer's guilt – *The Banquet* adds a new dimension to the narrative with stylized combat scenes and spectacular palace sets. Much in the same way as Zhang Yimou's recent historical *wuxia* films, everything in *The Banquet* is color-coded. Zhang Li's cinematography features scenes bathed in scarlet reds, underscoring the lust, betrayal and bloodshed in the story, while Wu Luan's innocence at the film's start is expressed in his ghostly white robes. And Tan Dun's rich full-orchestral and vocal score create a treat for the ears as well.

Director
Feng Xiaogang

Screenwriters
Qiu Gangjian
Sheng Heyu

Cinematographer
Zhang Li

Cast
Zhang Ziyi
Ge You
Daniel Wu
Zhou Xun

Running time
131 minutes

24

Although critically acclaimed internationally for his comedies like *Cell Phone* and *Big Shot's Funeral,* few were aware of Feng Xiaogang's work in the West and some saw *The Banquet* as his attempt to change this. With the combination of Zhang Ziyi – one of only a handful of Chinese actresses who have managed to break into Hollywood – stunning visuals and kung fu action, more people now take notice of Feng Xiaogang on the festival circuit. A new direction has begun in Feng's career and, rather than return to the comfortable arena of comedy, he has continued to expand his horizons, following this film with a gritty war movie (*The Assembly*), a romantic comedy (*If You Are the One*) and a tear-jerker of a disaster movie (*Aftershock*).

十七岁
的軍

Shiqi Sui de Danche

Beijing Bicycle
2001

The bicycle is an icon of Beijing. The city is so flat that a bicycle makes traversing the longest of distances manageable, even for the chronically unfit. But keeping hold of your bike in Beijing is notoriously difficult, as crafty thieves help themselves regardless of how good you might think your lock is. For Wang Xiaoshuai, an independent director from the so-called Sixth Generation, the bicycle is seen as a means of freedom and climbing the social ladder in *Beijing Bicycle*. The Chinese name for the film, *Shiqi Sui de Danche*, translates as "17-year-old's bicycle" and refers to the two 17-year-old main characters. They both believe that they own the bicycle in question and believe it has the power to improve their lives.

Guei is a country bumpkin, recently arrived in Beijing. He gets a job with a courier company – a big step up for a country boy used only to farming. What's more, the job comes with a sparkling new mountain bike, his as soon as he's completed enough deliveries. His bike is stolen while he makes a delivery to a bathhouse – a direct parallel to Vittorio De Sica's *Bicycle Thieves*, on which much of *Beijing Bicycle* riffs. Across the city, Jian, a high-schooler, purchases the stolen bike secondhand from a market after his father breaks his promise to buy him the one he so sorely wanted. Refusing to give up, Guei eventually tracks down the bicycle, locating the marking he had made under the saddle, and steals it back. A war erupts between Guei, who clings desperately to the bike, his most important possession, and Jian's mountain bike gang.

Director
Wang Xiaoshuai

Screenwriters
Wang Xiaoshuai
Tang Danian
Peggy Chiao
Hsu Hsiao-Ming

Cast
Cui Lin
Li Bin
Zhou Xun
Gao Yuanyuan
Li Shuang

Running time
113 minutes

The film is as much about the similarities between the two boys as their differences. Although one is from the countryside and the other from the city, they both have fallen in love – Guei with a girl he spies through a window, Jian with a pretty girl with whom he rides to school – and both fight strongly to keep hold of their bike as if it was their love. The bike becomes a symbol of the social (and literal) mobility required to survive in Beijing.

In commenting on this film, Wang spoke of his desire to make a legitimately Beijing film, spurning the high-speed car chases of Hong Kong movies in favor of bike chases, all confined to the quintessentially Beijing *hutong* alleyways. Where it succeeds most is in its realistic portrayal of a Beijing that is full of social anxieties and problems but also full of inhabitants with a humorous and joyful disposition.

Da Lu

The Big Road
1934

Sexuality has a curious place in early Chinese cinema. Flirtation was permissible, but feelings of desire – be they sexual or the innocent interactions between sweethearts – were subordinate to the collective good. So when a waitress, Dingxiang, falls in love with laborer, Luo, in *The Big Road*, their feelings have to take to be put on the back burner for the good of the country. Such political themes flourished in a film industry where the majority of the writers, directors and producers were leftist intellectuals who viewed filmmaking as the perfect medium for communicating their righteous ideals in a tumultuous political period.

Writer-director Sun Yu (*Little Toys*) received his film education at Columbia and New York Universities, and his films reflect his worldly style. Given the peculiarity of the Chinese film industry at the time, Sun's film contains themes intended both to pacify the Nationalist government – which needed films that promoted strong national unity – and also express his personal feelings about communism.

The plot of *The Big Road* is as allegorical as they come: a group of six laborers toil away building a road of great strategic importance to the Chinese army, which is at war with Japanese invaders. At a roadside restaurant, the workers meet a pair of lively waitresses, Dingxiang and Moli, who will experience the same political awakening as the others. The happy gang of workers is sidetracked when a rich landlord betrays the Chinese resistance by trying to delay the road's construction. When the laborers refuse to stop working, they are imprisoned and tortured by the landlord. Thinking

Director
Sun Yu

Screenwriter
Sun Yu

Cast
Jin Yan
Zheng Junli
Han Lan'gen
Li Lili
Chen Yanyan

Running time
104 minutes

quickly, Dingxiang and Moli plan the workers' escape and lead them to freedom…but, as with most protagonists in this era, their success is short lived. Hours after resuming work on the road, a Japanese bomb attack kills everyone but Dingxiang. In the film's eerie climax, Dingxiang envisions the group rising from the dead and continuing to build the road. The work of a Chinese patriot, it seems, is never done.

Sun Yu employs an unusual technique: *The Big Road* was filmed without sound, but songs and background noise were later dubbed in. Songs were of vital importance to the movement, and when they appear in the film, the lyrics scroll along the bottom in a proto-karaoke fashion. The aural theme, "Song of the Big Road" sung by Nie Er, remains popular to this day. Despite the weighty subject matter, there are moments of Three Stooges-esque slapstick, which add a lighter dimension to the film. Also noteworthy is Sun Yu's borrowing of socialist filmmaking techniques from China's northern neighbors in the USSR. In a sign of things to come, *The Big Road* was one of the first pre-PRC films to prominently feature masculine, sweaty, shirtless men toiling for the good of their nation.

Dawan

Big Shot's Funeral
2001

Chinese cinema attendance decreased markedly in the 1990s, so much so that the government took the unprecedented step of allowing the China release of 10 foreign films (usually American) each year. Parties on both sides of the Pacific were desperate for this: Hollywood wanted to break into new and emerging markets, while the Chinese domestic box office needed an invigorating cash infusion. When *Titanic* became the highest grossing film of all time in China (eventually surpassed by another James Cameron epic, *Avatar*), it became clear there was money to be made. Rather than just exporting films, US studios realized that co-productions with US and Chinese talent could create a products almost certain to succeed in China.

And so market forces brought together North American actor Donald Sutherland and Chinese favorite Ge You in Feng Xiaogang's *Big Shot's Funeral*. Sutherland plays Tyler, a big shot American director in Beijing to shoot a remake of Bertolucci's *The Last Emperor* in the Forbidden City. Tyler lacks the enthusiasm of his younger days and the film is in danger of going out of control and over budget. His personal assistant (Hong Kong actress Rosamund Kwan) is there to keep him in check and her bilingual dialogue bridges the gap between Tyler and the enthusiastic but calamitous Yoyo (Ge You), hired to film the movie's behind-the-scenes footage. Yoyo tells Tyler about the Chinese custom of a "comedy funeral" for those who die in old age, celebrating their longevity rather than lamenting their passing. The production company removes Tyler from the helm, and he asks Yoyo to give him a comedy

Director
Feng Xiaogang

Screenwriters
Feng Xiaogang
Li Xiaoming
Shi Kang

Cast
Donald Sutherland
Ge You
Rosamund Kwan

Running time
100 minutes

funeral before collapsing into a coma. Sheepishly, Yoyo begins to prepare for the big event. As the plans become grander and more expensive Yoyo brings on his friend, an enterprising promoter. Sponsorship deals for all aspects of the funeral are auctioned off to the highest bidders. There's just one problem: Tyler awakens from his coma.

Feng's tone remains ironic throughout – the child emperor swigs Coke between takes – yet shows Beijing's cultural treasures like the Forbidden City in all of their magnificence. In the hands of lesser artists, this black comedy could devolve into a farce. But Ge You and Feng Xiaogang are perhaps China's most successful actor-director team, and they are at the top of their game in this film. *Big Shot's Funeral* attempts to appeal directly to Western audiences, and Feng received advice from Columbia Tristar on how best to shape the film to their tastes while in production. Although it wasn't a monster hit in the US, it did pave the way for future international attempts at co-production, allowing more talent and money to flow across the Pacific.

Hei Pao Shijian

The Black Cannon Incident
1985

Huang Jianxin is often regarded as being of lower stature than his innovative Fifth Generation contemporaries, but such a dismissal is unfounded. While the Fifth Generation chose to focus on the past with films like *One and Eight* and *Yellow Earth*, Huang took aim at contemporary society. *The Black Cannon Incident* is a dark, biting satire of China's paranoid and overly bureaucratic systems, and their inability to adapt to the fast-pace of their own reforms.

The film opens one night during a torrential downpour with an unnerving score heightening the tension. Our hapless hero, Zhao Shuxin, is an important engineer and fluent in German. He is currently assisting a joint venture with his German counterpart, Hans. Zhao sends a telegram containing the seemingly innocuous phrase "lost black cannon", which the suspicious operator takes to be a secret code. The operator passes on the information to an old Party cadre, who initiates a sequence of events that will forever change Zhao's career. While the "black cannon incident" is under investigation, Zhao is removed from his post and cannot act as interpreter for Hans, who has recently arrived in China. An inexperienced travel agent is brought in to replace Zhao, but his lack of German proficiency creates more problems than it solves. Zhao, meanwhile, becomes embroiled in a Kafkaesque nightmare, his political and personal vulnerability highlighted by Huang's use of tense long shots and the ominous sounds of whirring industrial machinery and ticking clocks. Zhao's project moves full steam ahead, but when the designs are implemented in Germany,

Director
Huang Jianxin

Screenwriters
Zhang Xianliang
Li Wei

Cast
Liu Zifeng
Gerhard
Olschewski
Yang Yazhou
Gao Ming

Running time
94 minutes

一滴水折射太阳的光芒，一桩"黑炮"透视了一个大世界。黄建新由此攀上影坛的高峰。

黑炮事件

1985年获广电部优秀故事片奖；1986年获第6届电影金鸡奖最佳故事片等，获殊荣提名最佳导演及最佳故事片奖。最佳男主角提名；1987年获柏林卡年电影节最佳影片之作品。

时间：1985 年
编剧：李唯
导演：黄建新
摄影：王新生 冯伟
主演：刘子枫 高明

they cause a fatal industrial accident. When the true nature of the "black cannon" is revealed, it further underscores the incident's nonsensical nature – Zhao, an avid Chinese chess player, misplaced his "black cannon" piece in his hotel room while on a recent business trip.

Amazingly, *The Black Cannon Incident* was Huang's first film and he would go on to produce other films in areas that his contemporaries wouldn't consider. The sequel to this film, *Dislocation* (1986), is also worth checking out as it is one of a very, very small number of Mainland science-fiction films. In the film, Zhao (who has been promoted to the role of director), creates a robot doppelganger of himself to sit in for him at boring government meetings. His films – and the ideas they represent – made Huang hugely successful, but they also offered another, lighter alternative for filmmakers seeking to evolve and modernize the concept of the Chinese film.

Benming Nian

Black Snow
1989

Although Jia Zhangke and the other Sixth Generation Chinese filmmakers are sometimes called the "urban generation", Xie Fei – more adroitly categorized as a Fourth Generation filmmaker – was responsible for one of the best and earliest examples China's gritty urban films. But whereas Jia uses China's cities as laboratories for detached observation, Xie presents a more threatening picture of urban life in *Black Snow*, suggesting that we should fear rather than engage with the city.

Li Huiquan has recently been released from prison after serving time for assisting his childhood friend, Fork, in a revenge-motivated murder. With no immediate family to rely on, Li decides to make money by selling clothes in a stall at the local market. He soon comes into contact with a beautiful nightclub singer, Zhao Yaqiu (played by pop starlet Cheng Lin). Attracted by Zhao's seeming naivety, Li volunteers to walk her home from work every evening to protect her from the unseemly dangers of the city. As her popularity increases, Zhao develops a diva attitude. Work also presents Li with difficulties, when a black market dealer, Cui Yongli, attempts to get him to sell pornography. Li refuses and instead takes a trip to south China with Zhao. When he is reluctant to sleep with a prostitute provided by Cui, their relationship further deteriorates and Cui violently attacks Li. Childhood friend Fork escapes from prison and comes back into Li's life. Li is torn between wanting to look after an old friend and not wanting to fall back into a life of crime. As the narrative speeds towards its tragic

Director
Xie Fei

Screenwriter
Liu Heng

Cast
Jiang Wen
Cheng Lin
Yue Hong
Liu Xiaoning

Running time
107 minutes

conclusions, all the pieces of Li's life have been tainted or destroyed by the city.

The film hangs on a brilliant performance by Jiang Wen, someone who made the difficult transition from child actor to adult star look easy. We feel every hardship he goes through, keeping us enraptured up until the grim finale. Xie, too, is at ease as a director, presenting a bleak portrait of a murky and morally bankrupt Beijing. A lecturer at the Beijing Film Academy, Xie captures the pains of young adulthood better than most, and his portrait of the capital's dirty underbelly is all the stronger for it.

Mangshan

Blind Mountain
2007

Modern Chinese films are often forced to live parallel existences. Funding can usually be found outside of China, but if a film is to be granted a screening license – or allowed to compete at international film festivals – the final cut has to be approved by Chinese censors. This is where the confusion occurs. For his first film, *Blind Shaft*, director Li Yang didn't even submit his film for approval, knowing it would never make it past the script development stage. Because of this, Li was banned from filmmaking in China. Despite fears that he would have to work abroad to continue his work, he began work on *Blind Mountain* in 2007. Equally incendiary as his debut effort, it was produced with the "guidance" of the film bureau. This meant that, before a final cut reached our screens, several plot points were changed and cuts were made. The original version is still available through clandestine channels, but the edited version is still well worth watching.

Huang Lu was the only "professional" actor in the cast, but even she had not yet graduated from the Beijing Film Academy when the film started shooting. Huang plays Bai Xuemei, a recent university graduate looking to earn money to pay off her parents' debts and to help her brother get an education. When traveling in the mountains of Shaanxi in search of medicinal herbs to collect and sell, Xuemei meets a few strangers. Things begin innocently enough, but when Xuemei wakes up one morning, she finds that she's been drugged and taken captive to be sold as a bride. Nobody in this fiercely traditional community will allow her to leave,

Director
Li Yang

Screenwriter
Li Yang

Cast
Huang Lu

Running time
95 minutes

and her nightmare continues. Alone and newly married to the son of a peasant family, other bought brides in the town advise her to accept and adapt to the situation. Tense and full of emotional drama, the film moves towards a conclusion which (depending on the version you see) is either abrupt and violent or satisfying and just.

Li Yang once again focuses on the dark side of Chinese society and, although the film is set in the 1990s, the director seems to indicate that the acquisition of brides through force is something that continues to this day. The rural and remote areas of China, so often portrayed as quaint and hard-working in films, are here exposed as backward and potentially deadly, turning the well-worn socialist view of the happy, hard-working peasant on its head.

Mangjing

Blind Shaft
2003

One day in July 2001, a friend of documentary filmmaker and one-time actor Li Yang recommended he read Liu Qingbang's novella *Holy Wood*. He finished it the same day. The next day he read it again. On the third day, he contacted the author and bought the rights. So compelled was Li by this tale about China's mining industry, he knew it was a story he needed to tell. Gaining access to the often-illegal mines of northern China to research and shoot the picture was dangerous: Li had to expose himself to armed gangs, corrupt officials and a potentially deadly environment. His experiences led him to conclude that, as outrageous as the original plot of *Holy Wood* was, it would need to be drastically embellished to do justice to the realities of coal mining in China.

The film's chilling plot is as dark as they come. Two con artists – Song Jinming (Li Yixiang) and Tang Zhaoyang (Wang Shuangbao) – latch onto a naive worker. They convince him that they are looking for a third person to help obtain a lucrative coal-mining contract they had promised to a relative. Persuading the new worker to pretend to be their relative, they begin work at a mine. In their scam – which they have repeated so often – they kill a young man and make it look like an accident, then go to the owner of mine (usually illegally run) and extort compensation. This time, the partners stumble across the wide-eyed Yuan Fengming (Wang Baoqiang). The 16-year-old's resemblance to their first victim and his genuine innocence cause Song to question his plans. Tang, on the other hand, only cares about

Director
Li Yang

Screenwriter
Li Yang

Cast
Li Yixiang
Wang Shuangbao
Wang Baoqiang

Running time
92 minutes

the money he wants to earn for his family. Tensions between the partners flare and dramatic consequences ensue.

Li's greatest visual achievement with *Blind Shaft* is in his frighteningly realistic recreation of the illegal mines, based upon his actual experiences working in mines with migrant workers in Inner Mongolia, Hebei and Shanxi before shooting the film. The title, *Mangjing* (*Blind Shaft*), is an insightful comment on the industry's moral myopia in exploiting its workers at all levels. In his final and most significant departure from the novella, Li decided to replace the book's "happy ending" in favor of one that he felt more appropriately reflected the despair inherent in China's coal mining.

Langshan Die Xue Ji

Blood on Wolf Mountain
1936

Blood on Wolf Mountain is, at its heart, a brilliant and vital allegory for the Chinese people. Fei Mu uses the conceit of a pack of murderous wolves terrorizing a Chinese village to highlight the gradual encroachment of the Japanese army into China. A year after the film was made, the Second Sino-Japanese War broke out and it became necessary for China to join together to fight.

In 1948 Fei Mu would go on to direct *Spring in a Small Town*, perhaps the greatest Chinese film in history, but it was *Blood on Wolf Mountain's* starlet, Jiang Qing, who made the greatest waves. Jiang, who went by the name of Lan Ping during her acting career, became known as Madame Mao after she wed Mao Zedong in November 1938. After her days as an actress had passed, she still maintained a firm hold on the film industry. In her leading role as a member of the "Gang of Four", she helped supervise all film production during the Cultural Revolution. In *Blood on Wolf Mountain*, nothing in her angelic performance suggested what a dark future was in store for both her and China.

The film is best when it's at its simplest: presenting the naked fear of the villagers as the wolves set in. The blood-thirsty beasts had already claimed the lives of "chickens, goats...people" and it's up to the villagers to band together for their own protection. Alas, the film's greatest weakness is in its portrayal of the wolves themselves. The lackluster beasts come across as a little mangy and the vicious overdubbed howling makes them seem even less frightening. Six years later in America, Jacques Tourneur would direct *Cat People*,

Director
Fei Mu

Screenwriter
Fei Mu

Cast
Jiang Qing
Li Lili
Zhang Yi

Running time
94 minutes

having the revolutionary idea of hiding his poor special effects through darkness and shadows. If only Fei Mu had had the same idea, the wolves would have had a bit more bite.

The film's denouement sees Fei Mu move back to more comfortable directorial territory: a shootout punctuated by fast-paced editing and montage – an homage to the film's almost certain Soviet influences. *Blood on Wolf Mountain* is an interesting specimen of a film that brings to the surface the underlying fears of the Chinese populace at the time. Such a film should have angered the Japanese, who already had an armed presence in China by 1931, but they missed the film's symbolism entirely.

Lan Fengzheng

The Blue Kite
1993

Tian Zhuangzhuang's best films of the 1980s were epic in scope and dramatic in pallet. Focusing on the lives of China's minority groups, the Beijing native looked at aspects of China's landscape and culture not often committed to film with *The Horse Thief* and *On the Hunting Ground*. But the work often considered to be his greatest, *The Blue Kite*, is a much more personal reflection on growing up in the People's Republic of China. Although the film ends in 1966, just before the start of the Cultural Revolution, the specter of those crushing 10 years permeates the production. Whereas other filmmakers of the 1980s and 1990s chose to address the Cultural Revolution more directly, Tian skillfully alludes to it by examining the forces that brought it about through the eyes of a child.

The film is divided into three segments, each dealing with the death of a significant figure in the life of Tietou, the young protagonist, while also reflecting China's political development.

Tietou's parents are married shortly after the death of Stalin, when political ideology is beginning to creep into the personal life of every Chinese person. Tietou's father, Lin Shaolong, is just a simple librarian, but is swept up in the Anti-Rightist campaigns of the 1950s and punished for voicing his opinion on one of Chairman Mao's maxims. Being "anti-revolutionary" lands him in a labor camp, where he later dies. The news of his death arrives in the form of a letter, but Tietou is too young to read the message.

The second section of the film deals with Tietou's mother and her relationship with her husband's former colleague,

Director
Tian Zhuangzhuang

Screenwriter
Xiao Mao

Cast
Lu Liping
Pu Quanxin
Li Xuejian
Gao Baochang

Running time
138 minutes

Li. Devastated by the guilt of having a hand in sending Tietou's father to the labor camp, Li slaves away and gives all of his time, money and energy to Tietou's family. But the Great Leap Forward – a time when disease and starvation took countless Chinese lives – takes its toll, and Li dies of ill health.

Tietou's mother marries a government official to rescue her family from poverty. The union is loveless and, despite a fancy new house, the family unit functions poorly. In the run-up to the Cultural Revolution, Tietou's new stepfather is assaulted by a group of Red Guards, his heart gives way and he dies.

Growing up in the same era as Tietou, scriptwriter Xiao Mao drew upon his personal experiences in penning this story of a family whose fortunes were so intimately tied to those of the nation. Exceptionally shot and acted, *The Blue Kite* is heir to the strong tradition of reflective Chinese movies that so beautifully explore the anxieties and tragedies that China endured during the Mao era.

Liulang Beijing

Bumming in Beijing: The Last Dreamers
1990

Director Wu Wenguang was one of many prestigious graduates to hail from the Beijing Film Academy. But unlike his trailblazing peers who produced groundbreaking fictionalized pictures in the 1980s, Wu's innovations were in the realm of documentary filmmaking. *Bumming in Beijing: The Last Dreamers* is widely considered the beginning of the New Documentary Movement, a brand of filmmaking that arose in the wake of the Tian'anmen incident of 1989 and that focused on those individuals marginalized in Chinese society.

Wu Wenguang's lens is aimed squarely at five artists living in squalor around Beijing. All of them are originally from the provinces, but after graduating from Beijing universities in the mid-1980s they decided to stay in the capital. This decision to openly reject a traditional danwei (assigned work unit) was a new one in China at the time, and the artists' unusual lifestyles are explored in this film. As the curious title alludes, these "dreamers" appear particularly ethereal as talking heads in the "let everything hang out" style in which they are shot. These so-called artists appear much more focused on the day-to-day mundanities of existence than actually creating any art. Only Mou Sen, whom we see engaging in a stage-play reading, appears to be actively producing art. The artists are difficult to sympathize with, because they obsess with the "foreign market". To them, it seems, their artistic heritage is irrelevant. Creativity is merely a springboard to the outside world.

Director
Wu Wenguang

Running time
70 minutes

Wu's camera masks his feelings about his subjects. For him, the "dreamers" are interesting because they go against what's expected of them. Their rebellion – albeit self-righteous and self-interested – is an important one, especially when so much of the artistic community found themselves flung far away from Beijing in the wake of the Tian'anmen Square demonstrations and subsequent crackdowns. Wu caught up with all five artists several years later in his documentary *At Home in the World*. Unsurprisingly, all but one of them (Mou Sen) had married foreigners and moved away from China. *Bumming in Beijing's* importance today lies less in its subject matter, though, than its interesting new aesthetic, which created a new documentary film movement in China.

手机

Shouji

Cell Phone
2003

"Many Chinese directors make movies for the Cannes, Venice, or the Berlin film festivals," Feng Xiaogang once said in an interview. "But they don't think about whether their movies will appeal to audiences." Therein lies the beauty of a director who, unlike the art house princes and princesses in this book, makes films that the Chinese people themselves truly love. But Feng does not merely present some saccharine vision of China. His films are often as serious and insightful as they are slapstick. In *Cell Phone*, he focuses on the Chinese people's dependence on the mobile phone (a billion users and counting) and the device's potential to mislead.

The film opens in 1969, during the height of the Cultural Revolution, when all long-distance telecommunications went through overcrowded offices. A young couple journeys into town to contact a friend working in a mine. The effort needed to make what by today's standards is an easy call seems outrageous, but that is Feng's point. The benefits of connectivity that mobile phones have given us are huge, but we take them too much for granted.

Flash forward to 2003 and the toupeed Yan Shouyi (Ge You), a successful talk-show host who has committed a cardinal sin for an adulterer – leaving his cell phone at home. When his *ernai* (mistress) calls and his wife answers, the latter's suspicions are aroused. When Yan returns to pick up his phone, he dismisses her questioning as nonsense, and it becomes clear that the serial womanizer will have to keep lying to cover his tracks.

Director
Feng Xiaogang

Screenwriter
Liu Zhenyun

Cast
Ge You
Zhang Guoli
Fan Bingbing
Xu Fan

Running time
102 minutes

The always-watchable Ge You plays the weaselly philanderer with consummate ease, and it's hard to feel any sympathy for him as his web of lies begins to crumble around him. The film is dark, raising uncomfortable questions about Chinese attitudes toward extramarital affairs. The problem is so rife, in fact, that when the film came out in 2003, it allegedly ended a number of marriages, as women saw their husbands' intricate lies exposed through Yan Shouyi's antics.

Laogong zhi Aiqing

Cheng the Fruit Seller a.k.a. Laborer's Love
1922

Not the earliest Chinese film by any means – that honor rests with the 1905 short *The Battle of Dingjun Shan* – but *Cheng the Fruit Seller* is the oldest Chinese film that survives in entirety. It offers insight into street life in 1920s Shanghai, but its significance is more than just historical. The film is also a great yardstick for comparing the progress of Chinese cinema relative to those around the world. Slapstick humor was perhaps the most easily exportable genre at the time, with the great stars of the American silent era like Charlie Chaplin, Buster Keaton and Harold Lloyd keeping audiences in stitches around China. Lloyd's influence, in particular, was felt in Shanghai, and his short film *Never Weaken* (1921) appears to have inspired *Cheng the Fruit Seller*.

In the Chinese version of the well-worn plot, Cheng is infatuated with the daughter of an unsuccessful quack doctor, but his marriage proposal is rebuffed by the doctor because, as the intertitle states, "Only a man who improves my business can marry my daughter." Ever ingenious, Cheng comes up with the novel idea of injuring as many people as possible – via a trick staircase that he controls from below – to keep the number of patients in the doctor's incapable hands at a maximum. Fortune smiles and Cheng is granted the object of his affections.

Hardly a groundbreaking exposition, but the humor and energy of this 22-minute film is to be applauded. Compared to the work of Chaplin et al at the time, it was rather slapdash, and – apart from the setting – there isn't much to differentiate them. The actor's performances are influenced

Director
Zhang Shichuan

Screenwriter
Zheng Zhengqiu

Cast
Zheng Zhegu
Yu Ying
Zheng Zhengqiu

Running time
22 minutes

by Chinese theater, incorporating twisted expressions, mime and exaggerated gestures. The comedy is of wide appeal and doesn't require a great understanding of Chinese culture to enjoy. The themes of this film are believed to have been influenced by the May 4th Movement, in which China started to place greater importance on simple workers like Cheng rather than its intellectual elites, who were regarded as out of touch with the people.

The survival of the film is probably due to the increased professionalism in film production that began at the time in China. The Mingxing (Star) Company – founded in 1922 by pioneers Zhang Shichuan and Zheng Zhengqiu with accounts man Zhou Jianyun – realized the importance of maintaining a capable group of actors. They therefore formed their own film school and began cultivating the group of actors and filmmakers who would help establish Mingxing as one of the leading Chinese film companies until the end of the 1930s. Sensing the marketability of silent films abroad (no need for dubbing), the Mingxing Company produced intertitles of the film in English and Chinese. Perhaps they hoped to export *Cheng* to places like San Francisco, where it would have been well received by the local Chinese immigrant population.

Zhongguo

Chung Kuo – Cina
1972

Chung Kuo was made by the noted Italian director Michelangelo Antonioni and, as such, is a tenuous inclusion in this collection. But for those trying to understand what China was like during the Cultural Revolution – a period where the Middle Kingdom shut itself off from the rest of the world and tried to effect dramatic political and cultural changes – this film has no equal. Virtually every major Chinese director (Xie Jin, Zhang Yimou, Chen Kaige, et al) has attempted to capture something of the feeling of the time, but only Antonioni's camera was allowed to record its day-to-day life. The film – shot over an eight-week period by a crew that was never without Party minders – is not without limitations.

The film is divided into three parts mainly according to the locations that the director and his crew visited during their stay: Beijing, Shanghai and Suzhou. Antonioni provides a dulcet voiceover throughout the three-plus-hours long film. Antonioni is known for his free-form movies such as *Blow Up* and *L'avventura*, and trademark long takes. These shots – sometimes lasting several minutes – are use here to capture simple actions, like a group of factory workers discussing their day or an old man in a Mao suit painting pictures. Although made with a loose structure, the documentary is at turns fascinating and bleak. In an early scene, Antonioni literally lets it all hang out with a powerful shot of a woman receiving a caesarian section with acupuncture as her only anesthetic. Later, he shows us a troupe of acrobats going through a stunning juggling and wire-walking routine, but

Director
Michelangelo
Antonioni

Writers
Michelangelo
Antonioni
Andrea Barbato

Running time
207 minutes

"It's hard to accept the idea that the Chinese invented everything, including fettuccine."

there's something hollow about their made-up faces as they joylessly go about performing. Antonioni sees China through the eyes of a visitor, creating a tender portrait of its people rather than documenting its achievements.

But the drab environment and unimaginable uniformity, from the murky canals of Suzhou (which he, perhaps jokingly, compares to Venice) to the almost unrecognizably undeveloped Shanghai, must have angered the Chinese authorities when they saw it. Antonioni had been hired to record the China's "new life" and what he produced was a somewhat eerie travel diary focusing on few of its positive aspects. Mao Zedong and his wife Jiang Qing vehemently condemned the director and his film just a year after it was made, and Antonioni complained that his minders had tried to manipulate the action, never letting him shoot anything without their interference. Still, *Chung Kuo* is useful today as a window into China at a time when filmmaking had practically ground to a halt.

Fengkuang de Shitou

Crazy Stone
2006

Crazy Stone is the little film that could. This low-budget comedy that cost around 3 million RMB (about $375,000 at the time of production) was the surprise box office hit of 2006, beating off stiff competition from both home and abroad and taking in 23 million RMB. It wasn't just financial hurdles that it had to overcome to connect with audiences, but also linguistic ones – the majority of the dialog is spoken in a strong Sichuanese dialect, hard to follow for the majority of Chinese speakers. But the film's lack of pretension, and its conscious references to popular Western and Hong Kong movies, endeared it to domestic viewers.

A rare jade stone – which also serves as the magical MacGuffin – is discovered in a factory outhouse by the building's owner. The precious object restores his fortunes, and now he has the financial capability to resist an unethical developer intent on buying up the land. The presence of the highly valuable stone comes to the attention of three bumbling would-be thieves, who intend to steal it before the owner can put it up for auction. The only thing standing in their way is the factory's security guard, who is charged with protecting the stone. But they are not the only ones who want to get their hands on it, as the unscrupulous developer has hired a highly experienced and technically savvy cat burglar from Hong Kong to steal it. Even the factory owner's son is after the jade, because he believes that it will enable him to be more successful with women. The three groups are in direct competition, and their efforts are more often foiled by each other than the security guard. As the plans

Director
Ning Hao

Screenwriters
Ning Hao
Zhang Cheng
Yue Xiaojun

Cast
Guo Tao
Huang Bo

Running time
98 minutes

52

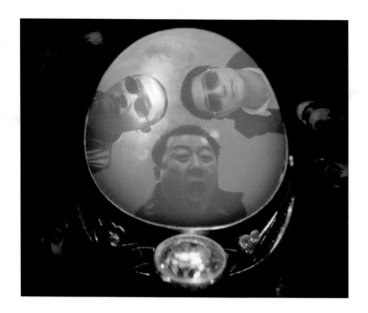

become more and more desperate, it becomes increasingly unclear who will end up with the stone.

Crazy Stone moved director Ning Hao from relative obscurity to the forefront of the Chinese film industry, and its success is attributed to his ability to appeal to Chinese comedic sensibilities. Although its dialect was difficult for the majority of the country to understand, the word play and puns, so characteristic of Chinese humor, still connected. In one example, quoted so often it has entered everyday parlance, a character refers to his BMW as a "*bie mo wo*" (literally, "don't touch me"). Besides its quick-witted dialogue, the film is also rich in the ever-popular slapstick humor and references that will keep cinephiles happy. *Mission: Impossible* and Hong Kong action flick *Infernal Affairs* (which starred one of *Crazy Stone's* producers, Andy Lau) are alluded to, but it's the film's originality and ability not to take itself too seriously that make it so refreshing an addition to contemporary Chinese cinema.

十字街頭

Shizi Jietou

Crossroads
1937

The distinct tone of *Crossroads* might not instantly resonate with Western audiences. The blend of comedy and tragedy is unique, combining a stock romantic premise (girl and boy hate each other then fall in love) with isolation, suicide and unemployment. The result is at turns humorous and disheartening, but the stoicism exuded by the young university graduates speaks volumes about the necessity for China to "carry on" regardless of the problems it faced at the time. The film is also notable for break from the 1930s' leftist mold, focusing on the problems of academics rather than the working class.

The characters in *Crossroads*, four friends in Shanghai, face the universal problem that confronts all graduates: they have no idea what to do with their lives. The unemployed Xu attempts to commit suicide, but his friends manage to stop him. Liu decides to join the Communists and fight against the Japanese. Zhao and Tang remain in Shanghai to pursue their dreams: Zhao wants to be a writer and Tang hopes to become a sculptor. But reality catches up with them. Zhao gets a job as a proofreader at a newspaper and Tang dresses windows for shop fronts. Zhao lives in a squalid apartment, several months behind on the rent. His room is separated from his neighbor's by a thin wall, shared with the stunning Yang (Bai Yang), who works in a cotton factory. They work shifts at opposite ends of the day, so never cross paths, but they do take issue with the unruly state in which each of them leaves the apartment and engage in a war – staining each other's clothes and breaking picture frames. Later, they

Director
Shen Xiling

Cast
Zhao Dan
Bai Yang
Lü Ban
Sha Meng
Yi Ming
Ying Yin

Running time
110 minutes

54

meet on a bus and, not realizing each other's identity, fall in love. But just as they get over their "hatred" and start a relationship, a newspaper article informs them that Xu has succeeded in killing himself. The news shocks them, but at this darkest moment they react with strength and optimism, and make a pact to join the war against the Japanese invasion.

Crossroads looks at the problems facing all young people in China, but its greater significance is as a reflection of its era. The war with Japan exacerbated the traditional urban problems of unemployment, housing shortages and disillusionment, and while contemplating these issues it's often hard to remember that the film was intended as a comedy. The romantic elements are more playful and helped to make Bai Yang one of the most popular stars of the '30s and '40s, going on to appear in such classics as *Eight Thousand Li of Cloud and Moon* (1947), *Spring River Flows East* (1947) and *Diary of a Homecoming* (1947).

Crows and Sparrows
1949

Wuya yu Maque

Director
Zheng Junli

Screenwriters
Chen Baichen
Shen Fu
Wang Lingu
Xu Tao
Zhao Dan
Zheng Junli

Cast
Zhao Dan
Wei Heling
Sun Daolin
Wu Yin
Shangguan Yunzhu

Running time
111 minutes

In 1948, around three-quarters of a million people packed into cinemas across Shanghai to see the film *The Spring River Flows East*. The sweeping drama, often called the "Chinese *Gone with the Wind*", proved less popular with the Kuomintang government, who took issue with its critical tone. From then on, the production company Kunlun Film and, in particular, the film's co-director Zheng Junli, were under close scrutiny from the Nationalist government. So much so that when they submitted a copy of the script for their upcoming picture *Crows and Sparrows*, they used a dummy copy that removed all portrayals of KMT officials as corrupt and idiotic.

Crows and Sparrows uses a Shanghai apartment building as a microcosm for what was happening throughout China during the last days of the civil war. The tenants of the house all hail from different social backgrounds and classes, but are all united in their hatred of their landlord, Hou Yibo. Hou, as it happens, is a high-ranking official in the KMT government and along with his mistress, Yu Xiaoying, supervises three families in the building. Hua Jiezhi is a timid but well meaning teacher who lives with his wife, Yuan Jiajin, and their daughter, Weiwei; Kong Youwen was the building's original owner, but he was forcibly relieved of it by Hou during the Japanese occupation; and Xiao is a simple man who lives by selling his goods on the street. The tenants learn that Hou intends to sell their home and flee to Taiwan, and they realize that they must find somewhere else to live. After first banding together in their quest, they must

56

go their separate ways. Hua believes he can find sanctuary at his school, but the headmaster – a KMT supporter – has Hua arrested on a trumped up charge of inciting a strike. Hua's wife Yuan thinks that forming an alliance with Hou is her only chance of survival and she attempts to seduce him, but is rejected. Hua's daughter becomes desperately sick and their only medicine – a bottle of penicillin – is sold by Xiao and his wife to purchase black-market gold. But the situation improves when Hou must leave for Taiwan, as Kong will regain his rightful residence. Hua's daughter also secures the medicine she needs to recover and, as the Spring Festival rings in another year, the residents agree to improve their ways to allow for a brighter future.

Luckily for the producers, by the time the film was released the Chinese Communist Party had come to power and this film was exactly what they were after.

Gui Zi Lai Le

Devils on the Doorstep
2000

The feelings of animosity between China and Japan go back hundreds of years, and movies inspired by their prickly relationship also go back quite a ways. During the period of Japanese occupation in the 1930s, Chongqing's Central Film Studio produced a slew of films with violently anti-Japanese themes like *Protect our Land* (1938) and *Eight Hundred Heroic Soldiers* (1938); the filmmakers in Shanghai, however, were under stricter control and were forced to sneak their messages inside allegorical tales like *Princess Iron Fan* and *Blood on Wolf Mountain*. When the Communists came to power in 1949, anti-Japanese war films became an integral part of their propaganda machine and a whole genre decrying the invading Japanese *guizi* (devils) was born.

Jiang Wen's addition to the canon marks a significant departure. As with his previous work, *In the Heat of the Sun*, which took a sentimental view of the Cultural Revolution, Jiang wanted to give a different perspective on the Sino-Japanese War, as he felt literature and cinema only ever portrayed the Chinese as the hapless victims of Japanese aggression.

Elegantly shot in black and white (employing a visual style that harks back to the work of Japanese director Akira Kurosawa), *Devils on the Doorstep* takes place in a small village near the Great Wall, during the final days of the Sino-Japanese War. Ma Dasan, played by Jiang himself, is a simple man who becomes unwittingly entangled in the Chinese resistance movement. One night, an unnamed man turns up at his door and demands that he keep two Japanese soldiers

Director
Jiang Wen

Screenwriters
Shi Ping
Shi Jianquan
Jiang Wen
You Fengwei

Cast
Jiang Wen
Kagawa Teruyuki
Yuan Ding
Jiang Hongbo

Running time
139 minutes

58

as hostages. Over the next couple of days, the village elders interrogate Kosaburo Hanaya (Kagawa Teruyuki), a fanatical Japanese sergeant, and Dong Hanchen (Yuan Ding), his subservient Chinese translator. The two men prove tough nuts to crack – especially as Dong intentionally mistranslates Kosaburo's spiteful diatribes against the villagers – and their captors begin to worry when the Chinese resistance fighter does not return. In a fit of panic, the villagers order Ma to execute the prisoners, which he is loath to do, so he instead takes them to the watch towers of the Great Wall. When Ma's plan is discovered, he is nearly killed by the villagers. They eventually relent, preferring to keep the captives alive, but over time they begin to fear that they will be discovered and seen as collaborators.

The resonating humor of Jiang's film does not hint at the storm it caused. Winning the Grand Prix at Cannes, the film was condemned and eventually banned by the Chinese government for "severely distorting history" and characterizing the Chinese as "ignorant...not hating the Japanese as they should". But in going against the grain, Jiang's film succeeds by finally presenting something more than a one-dimensional view of the war with Japan.

Zaochun Eryue

Early Spring in February
1963

The intricacies and social etiquette of Chinese society can seem baffling to outsiders. For the Chinese, maintaining a balance between outward "acceptability" and internal happiness is an age-old conundrum, but such psychological struggles are rarely represented on the big screen. *Early Spring in February* belongs to a select group of films, along with *Spring in a Small Town*, which concentrate on characters' inner turmoil rather than their positions within a collective. As such, both movies have been hailed by critics and academics alike for probing deeper than most contemporary Chinese movies. *Early Spring in February* was made in 1963 and could not escape the necessity of a pro-Communist slant. But here it is more subtly implied with a more general look at the "wrongs" plaguing society during the Kuomintang era.

An intellectual, Xiao Jianqiu, accepts an offer to teach at a school in a small town from his friend, Tao Mukan. At first glance, the town is idyllic; a close-knit and happy community. Xiao discovers that his best friend, Li, was killed whilst fighting in the Northern Expedition – KMT leader Chiang Kai-shek's military campaign to unify China. Xiao befriends Li's widow and begins financially supporting her family. Such altruistic behavior is greeted with great suspicion by the townspeople and Xiao becomes the subject of gossip. His only ally is Tao's younger sister, Ms. Tao, but her ambiguous support enrages her suitor, Qian. To retain respectability Xiao must choose between the impoverished Ms. Li or the beautiful Ms. Tao, for whom he really does have feelings. Placing virtue before his heart, Xiao marries Ms. Li, who he

Director
Xie Tieli

Screenwriter
Xie Tieli

Cast
Sun Daolin
Fan Xuepeng
Xie Fang
Shangguan Yunzhu

Running time
120 minutes

reasons would benefit most from the union. But nobility in pre-Communist times, the film tells us, does not lead to happiness. Li and Xiao's characters are viciously attacked by the community, and the loss of face causes the former to takes her life. All these characters have is their name, honor and dignity, and without them, nothing is worth living for. Staring at the wreckage around him, Xiao concludes that the only way to make a difference is to change society as a whole, which to him means joining the CCP.

Xie Tieli's film is based on the novel by leftist writer Rou Shi and although, like most films of the time, it portrays the "evils" of the society of the 1920s, it is unusual in that it portrays intellectuals in a positive light. Xiao is a noble man in smart clothes, who seeks to improve the lot of all those around him. But it seems there can be no defense, as the filmmakers would have us believe, from the inescapable dangers of immoral pre-Communist society.

Donggong Xigong

East Palace, West Palace
1996

"Do they have gay people in China?" is the sort of question that outsiders sometimes ask, and the answer is a resounding yes. Historically, records of same-sex relationships in China appear as far back as the Han dynasty (206 BC-220 AD), but in the 20th century *tongxinglian* (same-sex love) became a taboo subject. It disappeared entirely from academic books, and its prevalence was blamed on the "foreign influence" of the Manchus and Westerners. Today, despite more and more Chinese homosexuals becoming comfortable in their own skin, a conflict still exists with the rigidity of traditional Chinese society. Homosexual men are often unable (or unwilling) to accept the truth about themselves, a conflict that forms the spine of underground-filmmaker Zhang Yuan's *East Palace, West Palace*.

The film is named after the two parks at either side of the Forbidden City, cruising areas for Beijing's gay men. One evening a local cop whose job it is to keep the park clear of such men, Xiao Shi (Hu Jun), picks up Ah Lan, a young gay writer. Realizing that Ah Lan was the same man who had kissed him unexpectedly when he last "cleared out" the park, and later sent him a gift, Xiao Shi arrests and detains him for the night. A sexual Stockholm syndrome develops between the men, their confrontation oscillating between interrogation and seduction. Xiao Shi's anger, frustration and disbelief at Ah Lan and his lifestyle are almost tangible, but he is also clearly conflicted – is there something of an attraction between them? The film feels like a stage play, with most of the action taking place in real

Director
Zhang Yuan

Screenwriters
Wang Xiaobo
Zhang Yuan

Cast
Si Han
Hu Jun
Zhao Wei

Running time
90 minutes

time. The score adds an additional theatrical element, with the unmistakable screeching of Peking opera. The film's denouement, too, makes use of the Peking opera tradition of female impersonation.

Often referred to as the first Mainland Chinese film with a predominant homosexual theme, *East Palace, West Palace* is a daring work. Zhang, however, paid a heavy price for exhibiting the film at the Cannes Film Festival, having his passport confiscated after he returned from a trip to Hong Kong in 1997. This lyrical and moving film's importance cannot be understated. The controversy surrounding it, and all "banned" films in China, has ensured that its memory will live on.

Baqian Li Lu Yun he Yue

Eight Thousand Li of Cloud and Moon
1947

Comparisons between Chinese movies and their American contemporaries are often overly simplistic (this book has been guilty of this on more than one occasion), but there are more than a couple of similarities between *Eight Thousand Li of Cloud and Moon* and Preston Sturges' 1941 film *Sullivan's Travels*. They were created in different worlds with different messages for entirely different audiences, but they share a belief that art is the most powerful method of escapism. Sturges' protagonist in *Sullivan's Travels* learns the merits of film comedy as a way to help people emerging from the Great Depression and the beginnings of the Second World War. Similarly, Shi Dongshan's two protagonists learn that regional theater is perhaps the only way to keep happy the millions who have just survived Japanese occupation.

In the heat of the Sino-Japanese War, Lingyu (Bai Yang) is a young woman desperate to join a traveling theater group despite strong opposition from her family. Enraptured by the troupe's ability to mobilize the masses in support of the resistance, Lingyu travels around southern China, learning the craft and also lessons in life. Before long she has fallen in love with Libin (Tao Jin), the troupe's musical director. They stay on the road for a number of hard years and, by the time they arrive in Chongqing, Libin has become sick. While in Chongqing, Lingyu runs into her cousin, now an entrepreneur, who had been skeptical about her joining the troupe. He reveals that he has feelings for Lingyu, but she is adamant in wanting to remain with Libin, who she later marries. When the war ends, the troupe disbands and the

Director
Shi Dongshan

Screenwriters
Shi Dongshan

Cast
Bai Yang
Gao Zheng
Tao Jin

Running time
124 minutes

couple heads back to Shanghai, where they move into a mansion with Lingyu's uncle. Despite the initial ecstasy that comes with the end of the war, the couple grows disillusioned with the new order under the Nationalists. Libin becomes a teacher and Lingyu an investigative reporter, but her inquisitive nature riles her cousin, who has his fingers in a number of seedy deals. Already distraught about the current state of the society they fought so hard to protect, the final blow comes for the pair when Lingyu is struck by a car. She is rushed to the hospital, but the film ends on an ambiguous note, with viewers not knowing whether she survives.

Made two years before the Communists came to power, the film taps into the leftist dissatisfaction with the new Nationalist regime after the Sino-Japanese war. The poverty stricken theater troupe is far happier than the suddenly cash-rich society they entered into after the war, and, unlike so many films made after 1949, the film does not have the ability to comfort the viewer with the *deus ex machina* of the arrival of the Communist Party – an ending that was almost uniformly tacked onto films immediately following the revolution.

Bawang Bie Ji

Farewell My Concubine
1993

Farewell My Concubine is an epic tale of China in the 20th century as told through the eyes of two Peking opera stars. History is something of an obsession for the Fifth Generation of directors (see Zhang Yimou's *To Live*), and for director Chen Kaige this film was a way of exorcising the demons of the Cultural Revolution – a period personally painful for him.

The film covers a period of 50 years and follows the story of two men: Xiaolou and Dieyi. They first attend Peking opera school together as young children. Due to his feminine looks, Dieyi (then called "Douzi") is taught the *Dan* (female) roles, becoming adept at all aspects of female impersonation. After graduating from the strict and sometimes brutal academy, they assume stage names – Dieyi (Leslie Cheung) and Xiaolou (Zhang Fengyi) – and become the most celebrated performers in all of Beijing – particularly famous for their roles as the king and the concubine in the opera *Farewell My Concubine*. The effeminate Dieyi is in love with Xiaolou but his sexual feelings are not reciprocated. Xiaolou instead falls in love with a prostitute, Juxian (Gong Li), whom he eventually marries. A rift develops between the friends, and Dieyi descends into opium addiction. The politics of China over the following decades – with warlord infighting, Japanese invasion, the Communist rise to power and the Cultural Revolution – test them both. They somehow manage to keep performing throughout, but are unable to avoid betraying each other.

The film is a lavish spectacle full of emotion and symbolism. Peking opera is the epitome of Beijing culture

Director
Chen Kaige

Screenwriters
Lillian Lee
Lei-Bik Wa
Lu Wei

Cast
Leslie Cheung
Zhang Fengyi
Gong Li

Running time
171 minutes

and, by observing the performances and the treatment of its stars, we better understand the hardships endured in the capital between the 1920s and 1970s. The film also analyzes ideas of gender identity and sexuality through the character of Dieyi. Initially rejected from the opera school because of a superfluous "sixth finger", his mother cuts it off so that he may be admitted. As an adult, he is unable to distinguish between his concubine stage persona and reality, which inevitably ends in tragedy. Gong Li gives a spirited performance as a woman trapped between feuding partners, at the mercy of their art and whatever political faction wants to use their popularity as a weapon. The scenes set during the Cultural Revolution, where the actors and their troupe are forced to publicly condemn each other, are particularly heartfelt from director Chen Kaige, who was forced to denounce his own filmmaker father during that period. Winner of the Palme D'Or at the Cannes Film Festival, Farewell *My Concubine* paints Beijing as a beautiful city laced with sorrow.

THE OPERA

In the original Farewell My concubine *opera, Xiang Yu, king of the Western Chu state (232-202 BC) fights against Liu Bang to unify China. Liu surrounds Xiang's soldiers. Knowing that he will soon die, the king releases his favorite horse, but the animal refuses to leave. Liu requests the company of his favorite concubine, Yu Ji. Seeing that they are doomed, Yu Ji commits suicide while performing a sword dance, so that they may die together.*

Wu Duo Jinhua

Five Golden Flowers
1959

Director
Wang Jiayi

Screenwriters
Zhao Jikang
Wang Gongpu

Cast
Mo Zijiang
Yang Likun
Zhu Yijin
Wang Suya
Tan Shaozhong

Running time
105 minutes

We don't often think of 1950s China – when men and women alike wore baggy Mao suits – as a highly sexualized period, but a population of over a billion doesn't happen by accident. Judging by the near total absence of romantic themes in the movies of the time, however, you might be forgiven for thinking otherwise. One section of Chinese society for whom the romantic realm was not forbidden, however, was its ethnic minorities. *Five Golden Flowers* is about the lives and loves of the Yunnan Province's Bai ethnic minority. Along with romance, music and comedy, the film also emphasizes of the role of ethnic groups in the construction of a socialist China.

Ah Peng, the film's male lead, falls in love with Jinhua ("Golden Flower") at first sight. After impressing her with his horse-riding skills (the Bai are renowned for their horsemanship), the pair agrees to meet again in a year's time at the Butterfly Spring. Much of the film's start is dedicated to showcasing the "exotic" nature of the Bai people through their music and colorful garb. A year later, Ah Peng returns to the Butterfly Spring, but his desired Golden Flower is not there. Rather than taking this as rejection, he resolves to find the woman he loves. What follows is a subtle comedy of manners that highlights a genuine peculiarity of China: although there are some 700 Chinese surnames, the majority of people in the world's most populous country use only about 20 of them. So when Ah Peng sets off in search of Jinhua, it's not long before he finds one and then another and another, but not the one he wanted. The different Jinhuas

he meets exhibit the variety of jobs that men and women were expected to do during China's Great Leap Forward (which started in 1958): there's Jinhua the foundry worker, Jinhua the tractor driver, Jinhua the stockyard worker and, most unfortunately, Jinhua the shit collector (well, manure, more accurately). Ah Peng remains upbeat and while he is attending the wedding of another Jinhua, runs into his intended. The original Jinhua, it turns out, is head of an agricultural commune set up to increase production, a key facility used during the Great Leap Forward. The film ends by bringing together all five Jinhuas with their respective beaus at Butterfly Spring for a grandstand musical number.

The film's gentle and lyrical take on romance is pleasing to the eye, and it's also refreshing to see a 1950s film that idealizes the present – actually a period of great famine in China – instead of simply denouncing the past. It can be slightly condescending in its treatment of the Bai, but it is also a beautifully photographed memento of the people and their culture that shouldn't be missed.

Mei Lanfang

Forever Enthralled
2008

Chen Kaige is a born and bred Beijinger. His images of winding *hutong* alleyways in *Farewell My Concubine* have come to define how the outside world imagines Beijing. Chen also has a passion for the city's defining art form: Peking opera. *Farewell My Concubine*, a fictionalized account of two opera stars in a politically tumultuous era, became Chen's most critically acclaimed film internationally. After less critical success with later productions, Chen returned to the operatic world, focusing this time on a real-life star. Mei Lanfang redefined Peking opera and was the first of its practitioners to appeal to an international audience. A symbolic hero of the Chinese, he was a man who devoted his life to the art, and his biopic, *Forever Enthralled*, allowed Chen to reconnect with Beijing's rich past.

As the film opens, Mei (played by Yu Shaoqun in his debut role) struggles with the thought of quitting the Peking opera world. The stage is a tough place to earn a living, but it didn't take long for Mei to make a name for himself. What made Mei such a star was his ability to create new and distinctive movements, breathing new life into the operatic form. In a key scene, Mei has an on-stage "battle" with an established opera star, Swallow. Mei wins over the crowd with his expressive gestures. In the film's second act, Mei, now married, falls for a younger female opera performer, played by Zhang Ziyi. Finally the film looks at the Sino-Japanese War, when Mei refused to perform for the Japanese invaders. The film is shot throughout with delicacy and brightness, and the opera performances,

Director
Chen Kaige

Screenwriters
Chen Kaige
Yan Gelin
Chen Kuofu

Cast
Zhang Ziyi
Leon Lai
Sun Honglei
Qiu Rubai

Running time
146 minutes

as you would expect from Chen Kaige, are vibrant and engaging.

Peking opera and film have always been good bedfellows. China's first movie, *The Battle of Dingjun Mountain*, was a filmed opera performance. And in his life, Mei Lanfang made several notable appearances on celluloid. One of Russia's greatest directors, Sergei Eisenstein, was fascinated with Mei Lanfang's technique and filmed many of his performances. With this fawning biopic, Chen Kaige, like his predecessors, has helped to further preserve the memory of a great man and his art.

Zhao Le

For Fun
1993

"I've never been to Peking opera; it doesn't interest me," director Ning Ying once said of her hometown's celebrated art form and the basis of her film *For Fun*. Rather than take aim directly at the opera, the gaze of her camera instead focused on its elderly practitioners, who form a troupe in order to sustain the quickly vanishing culture of their city. Ning's documentary-style camera work has often been compared to that of the Italian neo-realists, presenting a bleak and unflinching view of contemporary society. But her films are often more upbeat than those depressing European creations. The Italian connection is more rightly traced to the time she spent there in the 1980s, as well as her work as an assistant director on Bernardo Bertolluci's *The Last Emperor*.

Han is a man uncomfortably moving into retirement, having recently handed over his job as a doorman at a Peking opera theater to two young men. Without work, his life is solitary and unfulfilling, and he finds the activities of other retirees annoying and pointless. At one point his outright scolding of a group of pensioners singing in the park drives away their audience. It's then that Han realizes that forming an amateur Peking opera group will fill the void left by his work. The group meets regularly but Han is unable to compromise his exacting ways and regularly bosses around the other members. It's only when Han realizes the true importance of what they are doing – having fun – that he can really begin to enjoy himself and their performances.

Director
Ning Ying

Screenwriters
Ning Dai
Ning Ying

Cast
Han Shanxu
He Ming
Huang Wenjie
Huang Zongluo

Running time
97 minutes

Apart from the lead, all of the film's performers were untrained actors. This lends a tremendous amount of authenticity to the film, in which the camera sits in on the scenes like a careful observer. The film takes us inside the world of Beijing's elderly community, a group that may be the last guardians of many aspects of a traditional culture currently under threat from China's rapid modernization. Still, the film is not thinly veiled social criticism. It is instead a keenly observed peek behind the curtain into the lives of ordinary Beijingers and those who attempt to preserve their city's heritage.

Jianguo Daye

Directors
Han Sanping
Huang Jianxin

Screenwriters
Chen Baoguang
Wang Xingdong

Cast
Tang Guoqiang
Jackie Chan
Zhang Ziyi
Jet Li
Vivian Wu
Chen Kaige
John Woo
Stephen Chow
Feng Xiaogang
Ge You
Andy Lau
Tony Leung Ka Fai
Teddy Lin
Donnie Yen
Zhao Wei

Running time
138 minutes

The Founding of a Republic
2009

The Founding of a Republic may not present a nuanced view of the Chinese Civil War, but it perfectly illustrates the history of the last 60 years in Chinese filmmaking. The epic production contains many characteristics that have come to define filmmaking in China since 1949 and also hints at the future direction of the industry. It addresses very familiar subject matter in covering the years that preceded the Communist Revolution, but this film is not only a piece of propaganda intended to inspire love for the motherland, it is also a big-budget affair designed to maximize box office returns.

Han Sanping, co-director of the film and chairman of the state-owned China Film Group, is one of the most powerful men in the Chinese film industry. When the idea struck him to create a film as a "gift" to China, he assembled a cast to die for. Seemingly every major Chinese star – from the Mainland, Hong Kong and Taiwan – was queuing up to be in this picture. A total of 172 A-listers made cameos in the film, from one-time dissident directors like Chen Kaige to action supremos like Jet Li and Jackie Chan. Only in China could such a large-scale, coordinated effort come together.

The leading role of Mao Zedong is played by veteran TV actor Tang Guoqiang, best known for his frequent portrayals of the Great Helmsman. The film starts in 1945, at the end of the Second World War, as Mao and his plucky (at least that's how they are portrayed here) bunch of Communists try to overcome the Nationalist government. Rather than merely vilifying the Nationalists, the film is *relatively* even

handed in its portrayal of Chiang Kai-Shek and the events
that led up to the revolution. The production is a largely
sedate affair, composed of scenes and characters (who pop
up and disappear at an alarming rate) repeatedly spouting
Communist ideology in the lead up to the decisive battle.

While *The Founding of a Republic* made no waves at
cinemas around the world, it did hint at the role the Chinese
government was going to continue to have in filmmaking.
The early 2000s saw a large number of high-profile Chinese
films banned, and patriotic efforts like *The Founding of a
Republic* showed how the government could still use all
resources at hand to project and manipulate China's image.

Jidu Hanleng

Frozen
1996

Wang Xiaoshuai is a filmmaker who truly deserves the mantle of "underground director". Fresh out of the Beijing Film Academy, he scrounged film stock, had to let his entire cast and crew go unpaid and – legend has it – existed on a single meal a day for weeks to complete his first film, *The Days*. The film focused on the deteriorating relationship between two artists during the tough period following the Tian'anmen Square massacre in 1989. It was selected by festivals overseas, but landed Wang in hot water with the Chinese authorities. The Film Bureau blacklisted Wang, making it impossible for him to receive funding for future films. Tenacious as ever, Wang went ahead and started work on his next feature under the pseudonym "Wuming" (literally, "no name") to avoid trouble.

With a slightly larger budget than his previous effort, Wang shot *Frozen* in color and hired Jia Hongsheng and Ma Xiaoqing – two of the most important actors of their generation – to star in the film. Although initially wanting to move away from the art scene, Wang found himself drawn to the "true story" of a performance artist, whose final artistic piece was to kill himself. The idea was so intriguing to Wang – who later discovered that the artist hadn't in fact killed himself for artistic reasons – he decided to use it as a basis for his film.

Frozen was originally entitled "The Big Game" to reflect the dangerous nature of some avant-garde performance art. Jia Hongshen plays Qi Lei, an artist whose work focuses on death. After experimenting with the simulation of death

Director
Wang Xiaoshuai

Screenwriters
Pang Ming
Wang Xiaoshuai

Cast
Jia Hongsheng
Ma Xiaoqing

Running time
111 minutes

in two "acts", Qi decides that, on the longest day of the year, he will melt a block of ice with his own body, consequently killing himself through hypothermia. The act, he says, is a protest of the coldness of society. The final scenes of the film, along with an earlier one in which the artist eats soap, are excruciatingly hard to watch. Wang admitted that he feared for actor Jia Hongshen's safety while filming the final scene and sent him to hospital for a checkup afterward.

The film – and the protagonist's fate – is cruelly ironic. Wang has stated he made the film to offer support for the performance art community in China, who were getting more support overseas than they were at home. *Frozen* also proved that Wang, despite the government's attempt to silence him, was a consummate director destined to become a leading light of Sixth Generation Chinese filmmaking.

湘
女
萧
萧

Xiang Nü Xiaoxiao

A Girl from Hunan
1986

Xie Fei was a man well acquainted with the art of cinema. After graduating from the Beijing Film Academy's directing department in 1965, he continued lecturing there for the next several decades. His work as a film critic is highly regarded, but he is best known for the movies he directed in the '80s and '90s, when he and other Fourth Generation directors began to reflect on the cultural issues most affecting China. Along with Wu Lan, Xie Fei chose to look at the traditional practices and rituals in Hunan (Chairman Mao's home province), especially those which were antithetical to the advancements being made in other areas of Chinese society. *A Girl from Hunan* examines one such custom: marrying off a fatherless infant male to an adolescent female. These strange betrothals involve a young girl raising her future husband, from diapers to the bedchamber.

This is the situation that befalls Xiaoxiao, a rosy-faced teenager entering into an arranged marriage with Chunguan, a toddler. Their interactions are intriguing to anyone with a cursory knowledge of Freudian psychoanalysis: Xiaoxiao nurses, tends to and refers to her future husband as Didi (little brother). Oedipal fires have surely been lit for the innocent Chunguan, but for Xiaoxiao, it is the abrupt arrival of her own sexual awakening that causes the most trouble. Xiaoxiao meets and falls in love with Huagou, a hired laborer working for her mother-in-law, starting a forbidden affair with an element of danger – one local woman in the village is executed for adultery. The situation takes an unfortunate turn for the pair when Xiaoxiao discovers that she is

Directors
Xie Fei
Wu Lan

Screenwriter
Zhang Xian

Cast
Na Renhua
Ni Meiling
Liu Qing
Deng Xiaoguang

Running time
93 minutes

pregnant, and the only available course of action is to flee. Huagou – no prince charming – deserts her, leaving Xiaoxiao no option but to try and make off on her own. Her flight is short-lived: she is caught and returned to her mother-in-law, who decides to spare her life, because killing her would only result in a vengeful ghost haunting the family.

The film flashes forward to when Xiaoxiao's child is now a few years old and the time has come for Chunguan to finally consummate the marriage. The rural village prepares for two marriages: Xiaoxiao and Chunguan's and also for Xiaoxiao's toddler son, who will continue the tradition. The prospect is sickening to Chunguan, who flees the village.

Female sexuality and desire are here framed in a rural setting, thus the social critique is aimed less directly at the Han "masses". But Xie Fei's point is clear: for all the social advancement that was beginning to materialize, there were still fundamental problems with China's patriarchal traditions, which saw women as second-class citizens or even prisoners of their families.

Shennü

The Goddess
1934

"It's a bright, guilty world," said Orson Welles in *The Lady from Shanghai*, referring to the internationally renowned city of exoticism and sin that was Shanghai in the 1920s and '30s. And amongst the bright lights of this morally bankrupt city, a nameless prostitute (Ruan Lingyu) is forced to ply her trade in *The Goddess*. In this film, prostitution is (as it was in many of the films of the Golden Era) a symbol of oppression and victimization, and its tragic star, Ruan, plays the virtuous victim of society's double standards.

Whilst turning tricks in downtown Shanghai, Ruan is chased by a local policeman. In her bid to avoid detection, she hides in the home of a rotund gambler, but, in return for her safety, the gambler (Zhang Zhizhi) becomes her pimp. The money that Ruan used to collect for her son's education now cushions the coffers of the debaucherous gambler. But Ruan's suffering is not over: after managing to squirrel away enough money to pay for her son's school fees, the other students' mothers, objecting to her profession, petition the school's principal. The kind principal takes pity on the single mother and, after the boy's expulsion, resigns his post. Later, when Ruan discovers that her secret cash reserves have been raided by the drunken gambler, she strikes and kills him with a bottle. Convicted of murder, Ruan is jailed for 12 years, her only solace coming from the school principal, who promises to take care of her son. Alone in her cell, the final seconds of the movie see Ruan fantasizing about her son's future.

In telling the archetypal "hooker with a heart of gold" story, the Lianhua Film Company emphasized cinematography

Director
Wu Yonggang

Screenwriter
Wu Yonggang

Cast
Ruan Lingyu
Zhang Zhizhi
Li Keng

Running time
85 minutes

above over-the-top acting: sweeping camera shots and sparse use of intertitles enhance the highly visual style of this sophisticated melodrama. The breakthroughs in sound recording did not impact Chinese cinema as early as they did in other countries. Converting theaters and the added production expenses were not options for most Chinese producers, so many of the films remained silent throughout the 1930s.

Melodrama, particularly of the most tragic kind, was lapped up by Chinese audiences during this period. Despite the backlash against *The Goddess* at the start of the Cultural Revolution, the leftist cinema of the '30s has endured to this day. Director Chen Kaige (*Farewell My Concubine*) cites this movie as his personal favorite and such praise is not unduly given. *The Goddess*, despite its preachy tone, stands with the best work being produced around the world at the same time, and can rightly be considered the finest film of the China's Golden Era.

LIANHUA

Founded in 1930 by cinema mogul Luo Mingyou, Lianhua Film Company was a highly powerful organization with close ties to the Nanjing government. It was also a company of lofty ideals, its manifesto declaring that it wanted to "elevate art, promote culture, enlighten the masses and rescue China's film industry from degeneration and deterioration."

The Go Master
2006

Wu Qingyuan

Director
Tian Zhaungzhuang

Screenwriters
Ah Cheng
Zhou Jingzhi

Cast
Chang Chen
Sylvia Chang
Akira Emoto
Nishina Takashi

Running time
104 minutes

Like the game taking center stage in Tian Zhuangzhuang's *The Go Master*, the film is sedate, measured and controlled with rigorous precision. The narrative, even when at its most dramatic, is restrained to the point of solemnity. Tian's intense attention to detail helps paint a rich and insightful portrait of the legendary Go player Wu Qingyuan. Go is a game which started in China but reached the height of its popularity in Japan, and the film is as much about the often fractious relationship between these countries as it is about the relationship between the game and one of its greatest players.

Wu Qingyuan learns to play Go from his father at the age of seven. Realizing that the boy is no ordinary player, his family moves to Japan, where his skills can be nurtured in a Go academy. Wu, or Go Seigen as he is known in his adopted homeland, begins to compete professionally and thinks he has found his calling. External circumstances begin to impinge upon his playing, as the Japanese invasion of China, which began in the 1930s, causes tensions to rise. His tutors believe he will assume Japanese citizenship, but Wu, demonstrating monastic dedication, is more concerned with the game than with nationalism. Fearing retribution, Wu's family heads back to China, but he remains in Japan.

Wu meets the love of his life, Kazuko (Ayumi Ito), after joining a messianic cult and his passion for the game begins to wane. His religious leader, a woman called Jiko, hopes he will use the game to promote the cult's beliefs, and his teacher (Akira Emoto) also hopes he will again compete.

Emotionally adrift, he gives up the game for a time, but eventually resumes playing after leaving the cult at the end of the Second World War. Throughout his life, he struggles with illness (both mental and physical), but remains the undefeated Go champion for 17 years.

Watching the film requires patience from the viewer, but *The Go Master* is well worth the effort. Central to the film is the performance of Taiwanese actor Chang Chen as Wu. He dominates every scene with his low-key but intense presence, illustrating beautifully the mental devotion required to play Go at the highest level. While his world is swept up in a political maelstrom, Wu and his game form a calm center.

Beijing Nizao

Good Morning, Beijing
1991

Zhang Nuanxin graduated from the Beijing Film Academy in 1962 and first impacted Chinese film as a critic. Hamstrung by politics like many of her generation, it wasn't until many years later that she was able to make her directorial début. In her seminal essay, "On the Modernization of Film Language", co-authored with husband and renowned film critic Li Tuo, Zhang championed the development of a new cinematic language in China, which deviated from simply "putting pictures" to literature. This new approach instead focused on cinematography, narration and *mise-en-scène*, and took into account the developments in film criticism abroad. In many ways, that essay became the artistic manifesto for Fourth Generation directors. When Zhang finally got her opportunity behind the camera in the early '80s, her avant-garde work and exemplified the theories she had put forward. *Good Morning, Beijing* is not, however, an experimental film. Made after Zhang spent a period in France studying cinema, it is instead a portrait of the everyday lives of Beijingers and is most remarkable for its optimism.

The film opens on a typical frosty Beijing morning. Ai and Wang are bus conductors who regularly bike to work together. Wang is efficient and dedicated, while Ai is apathetic, paying little attention to her passengers' questions. As he obviously holds a candle for Ai, Wang's jealously is aroused when a new bus driver, Zou, arrives on the scene and Ai prefers to ride with him instead of Wang. They begin dating, but their differences and the fleeting nature of their attraction become apparent one day while

Director
Zhang Nuanxin

Screenwriter
Tang Danian

Cast
Ma Xiaoqing
Wang Anquan
Jia Hongsheng
Jin Tiefeng

Running time
100 minutes

window-shopping. Ai wants to quit her job and buy new clothes, while Zou believes she should work hard and stick with her current job.

Ai's attentions shift to Chen Mingke, a slick overseas student who wines and dines her at cheesy nightclubs around town. Ai is seduced by the fancy presents Chen gives her, from a gold necklace to a (rather comical by today's standards) boombox. Ai's old life and friends begin to drift away, but when she discovers she is pregnant, she finds out that her dream man is not what he seems. Chen is not an overseas student, but just a businessman playing an act to pick up women.

The film ends with a chance reunion between the characters a few years later aboard the number 99 bus. Ai, now married to Chen, is laden with shopping bags and is helped aboard by Zou and Wang. As the film closes, we are left to contemplate the different paths life takes, especially in a metropolis like Beijing, which can bring good fortune and pain in equal measures.

85

大闹天宫

Da Nao Tiangong

Havoc in Heaven
1961; 1964

The Wan brothers were just finding their feet when they made the country's first animated feature, *Princess Iron Fan*, but they produced a work of immense maturity with *Havoc in Heaven*. Rather than copying the Disney style, *Havoc in Heaven* has a feel entirely of its own. It borrows from traditional Chinese art, yet uses innovative techniques to create stunning scenes of heavenly delights and monkey mischief. As with *Princess Iron Fan*, *Havoc* takes its story from *Journey to the West*, this time focusing on an early chapter, where the monkey king Sun Wukong rebels against the Jade Emperor of Heaven. The film was produced in two parts, the first released in 1961 and the second in 1964. They were screened together for the first time in 1965, but soon after this the Cultural Revolution ground all screening and production of animated films to a halt.

The first part of the film consists of Sun Wukong searching for a weapon strong enough to withstand the Jade Emperor's vigorous attacks. An older monkey in his clan suggests that he might be able to find such a weapon with the Dragon King of the Eastern Sea. Sun dives to the bottom of the ocean and asks the Dragon King for a weapon, and is presented with a number of unsuitably weak spears and swords. He finally finds the pin used to hold down the sea during great floods, which turns out to be an enchanted staff. With this weapon, the Monkey King goes off in search of trouble. The Jade Emperor summons Sun to heaven to offer him a job, but the monkey cannot be controlled and soon returns to his mountain. In the second part of the film, told

Director
Wan Laiming

Screenwriters
Li Kuero
Wan Laiming

Running time
113 minutes

with spectacular visuals, the Jade Emperor and his servants take further steps to stop the Monkey King.

The film is an incredible, psychedelic experience. Vibrant colors flash at every turn. The characters look like they were plucked from the statues and murals in temples across China, only here they come to life, dance and explode across the screen. The film uses a Peking opera score, with every leap, crash and collision sounded out on traditional drums, cymbals and strings. For the Wan brothers, completing this film was a great achievement. They had hoped to start work on it as soon as their first feature was complete, but it took them many years and the result was well worth the wait. Had it not been for the ensuing "lost" decade that followed its release, they might made many more. Some see the film as a jibe at the Great Helmsman, with Mao as the irascible monkey, oblivious to the havoc he causes in his kingdom.

HAVOC

Since the film came out, the term "havoc in heaven" (da nao tiangong) has become slang for someone causing trouble or making a mess of something.

Yingxiong

Hero
2002

For his first foray into the martial arts genre, Zhang Yimou decided to cast a number of Hong Kong kung fu regulars (including Tony Leung Chiu Wai and Maggie Cheung) alongside the Mainland's most famous action hero, Jet Li. Many doubted the visionary director's ability to make an impressive *wuxia* flick, but the film proved to be a watershed for Zhang. Its large-scale release in America (financed by long-time admirer Quentin Tarantino) allowed Zhang to finally attract audiences at the multiplexes as well as the art houses. But attention of the entirely unwanted variety also reared its ugly head, as many critics saw the movie as a symbolic justification of totalitarian regimes; quite a change of pace for a man who had previously been considered a dissident filmmaker.

Zhang's process as a filmmaker is unique. In particular, during the scripting phase of *Hero* he chose a story and an all important color scheme before deciding upon a historical setting. Wanting to depict an imposing black palace, Zhang Yimou decided to base the film loosely on the legend of Jing Ke in the Kingdom of Qin (around 246-221 BC) – a time in which black palaces would most likely have existed. Jet Li stars as Nameless, prefect of a small district, who arrives at the gates of the King of Qin's (Daoming Chen) palace requesting an audience with the king. The king, driven to intense paranoia by repeated assassination attempts, has removed every object and person from the palace. He only allows Nameless to enter within 100 paces of him because he believes that the most dangerous potential assassins

Director
Zhang Yimou

Screenwriters
Feng Li
Wang Bin
Zhang Yimou

Cast
Jet Li
Tony Leung Chiu Wai
Maggie Cheung
Zhang Ziyi
Daoming Chen

Running time
107 minutes

"You have removed a great peril for me. How shall I reward you?"

have been eliminated – Nameless presents the king with the weapons of the assassins Flying Snow (Maggie Cheung), Broken Sword (Tony Leung) and Long Sky (Donnie Yen). The film recounts the stories (via flashbacks) of how Nameless dispatched them all. A twist comes at the end of the film when we learn that Nameless is in fact an assassin sent to kill the king, but he eventually decides to renounce his mission and dies for the greater good of a unified China.

Fight coordinator Tony Ching brings a depth of experience from his Hong Kong movies, but its Zhang Yimou's touches that stand out most. The sheer physical presence of the hordes of people in *Hero's* battle scenes is something no fight team or computer-generated imagery could hope to replicate. Virtually every scene has its own color pallet, and the film's structure revolves around these choices. Often dismissed as nothing more than a kung fu film, *Hero* respects the genre's conventions while also transcending them through Zhang's unique cinematic vision.

Furong Zhen

Hibiscus Town
1986

Hibiscus *(noun)*: a tropical plant or bush with large brightly colored flowers.

In Xie Jin's *Hibiscus Town*, there's one flower that surpasses all others: Hu Yuyin (Liu Xiaoqing). Along with her beauty and brains, Hu is a shrewd businesswoman, who opens a highly successful tofu restaurant. All this would be fine and dandy if it weren't for the Cultural Revolution, a time when personal grudges were easily avenged through politics and twisted psychology, and it was possible to persecute almost anyone with little pretext. Li Guoxiang is the man in charge of the local government-run canteen and is incensed by Hu's success, particularly by the new home she purchases with her earnings. During one of the political campaigns that occurred with frightening regularity during the 1960s and '70s, Li leads an investigation into Hu's business and brands her a "rich peasant". The loss of face for Hu and her family is so great that her husband takes his life. The Communist officials supportive of Hu are removed from their posts and replaced by the idle and incompetent Wang Qiushe. Hu is sentenced to perform manual labor with a convicted rightist, Qin Shutian, and over time they develop a bond that blossoms into a love sealed with a secret wedding. When Hu becomes pregnant, they must seek permission to marry from a party official, but Wang deems that they had an illicit affair and sentences Qin to 10 years imprisonment.

With the death of Mao Zedong, the Cultural Revolution ends and Qin is released. He reunites with Hu and the couple

Director
Xie Jin

Screenwriters
Zhong Acheng
Xie Jin

Cast
Liu Xiaoqing
Xu Songzi
Jiang Wen
Zhang Guangbei
Zhu Shibin

Running time
164 minutes

– thanks to the radical change in policy – is able to reopen the tofu restaurant.

Much has been written about Xie Jin and his films in this book, and he deserves every single word of praise. His mastery at directing actors – Liu Xiaoqing and Jiang Wen are both outstanding in this film – is testament to his rich stage background, and the film's somber tone is elevated by his passion for storytelling. Of the films produced in response to the Cultural Revolution and its consequences, *Hibiscus Town* is perhaps the finest example. To see the film is to understand the pressure, pain and fear that an entire nation lived through for a decade and also, for director Xie Jin, a deeply personal reflection on a time when his career was forcibly put on hold.

Dao Ma Zei

The Horse Thief
1986

China's ethnic minorities aren't often portrayed with depth on film, but director Tian Zhuangzhuang broke with tradition, beginning his career with films like *On the Hunting Ground* and *The Horse Thief*. Other directors of the era were dealing with the aftermath of the Cultural Revolution with the so-called "scar" films, but Tian wanted to address the deeper and more fundamental issues he felt films like *The Legend of Tianyun Mountain* were ignoring. *The Horse Thief* is a largely wordless film set in the expanses of the Tibetan plateau. Tian, using a style influenced by the work of Japanese director Akira Kurosawa and French New Wave directors like François Truffaut, frames a loose narrative around spectacular shots of some of China's most breathtaking natural surroundings. Even when capturing a traditional Tibetan sky burial, where the deceased is hacked to bits and fed to vultures, the film is visually arresting.

Religion is central to the people of Tibet and is the central focus in this narrative about a family's struggle for survival. Rorbu is a man of genuine faith, a Buddhist who dutifully worships the mountain god. When he steals a horse to provide for his wife and son, the whole family is exiled from the tribe. Rorbu's son becomes sick and dies, scarring Rorbu and his wife. In the hope of finding forgiveness from Buddha, they prostrate themselves in front of his image 100,000 times and perform various other rituals. Their devotion is seemingly rewarded when his wife gives birth to another son, but life remains tough and sickness spreads across the community. The hard times force Rorbu back into

Director
Tian Zhuangzhuang

Screenwriter
Zhang Rui

Cast
Tseshang Rigzin
Dan Jiji

Running time
88 minutes

crime. As the bitter Tibetan winter sets in, the family tries to return to the community before their path is blocked by the snow. Meanwhile, Rorbu is chased by the owners of the horses he has been stealing. The film closes with a shot of his abandoned knife next to bloodstained snow.

The film is visual poetry, the beauty of the images taking center stage over dialogue and narrative. By elaborately depicting Tibetan religious practices, Tian discusses the relationship between man and the gods, and also the fragile nature of life. The moral choices that Rorbu makes to survive may seem straightforward, but for someone so devout they weigh heavily on him.

The film was shot with Tibetan actors speaking the local dialect, but due to censorship laws at the time, it had to be dubbed into Mandarin before its release. Under the belief that the original dialogue would be reinstated soon after completion, Tian hastily recorded a rough vocal track. Unfortunately for him, it was never replaced, but, luckily for us, the dialogue is so sparse that it doesn't affect the incredible imagery.

Shimianmaifu

House of Flying Daggers
2004

There are three kinds of people attracted to the work of director Zhang Yimou. Some look back at his early work, when the director was "good" and making morose films like *Red Sorghum* and *To Live*; there are those who saw Zhang's choreographed opening ceremony for the 2008 Olympic Games in Beijing, astounded by the sight of 2,008 drummers beating in harmony; and finally there are those who discovered the leading figure of China's Fifth Generation filmmakers in the director of kung-fu epics like *Hero* and, most spectacularly, *House of Flying Daggers*.

The main question posed by those who cherish Zhang's earlier works about his more recent, (dare we say) more fun, output is: "How could a director who once challenged the rigidity of Chinese society and filmmaking practices now be so comfortably nestled within the mainstream?" Detractors, however, have no grounds for complaint. *House of Flying Daggers* is the work of a director moving into middle age with vibrancy, vitality and a visual style that few in the world could hope to match.

The film is set towards the end of the Tang Dynasty (859 AD), when a rebel group known as the House of Flying Daggers is redistributing the wealth of the corrupt and rich to the poor and needy – much to the chagrin of the local police force. The intricate plot, loaded with twists, sees Mei (Zhang Ziyi), a blind dancer at a local brothel and secret member of the Daggers, lead police captains Jin (Takeshi Kaneshiro) and Leo (Andy Lau) deep into the thick foliage of a forest in search of the rebel headquarters. But nothing is as

Director
Zhang Yimou

Screenwriters
Feng Li
Bin Wang
Zhang Yimou

Cast
Zhang Ziyi
Takeshi Kaneshiro
Andy Lau

Running time
119 minutes

"I thought you were hot as fire. In fact you're cool as water."

it seems. Allegiances, both old and newly formed, are tested and as Jin and Mei fight their way northward, the enemies fall in love. Zhang Ziyi's performance as the deadly Mei is skillfully played, and the role (along with her performance in *Crouching Tiger, Hidden Dragon*) cemented her status as China's most popular leading lady of her generation – in the West, at least. Kaneshiro plays a character who transitions from obnoxious drunk to dutiful leading man and similarly fulfills his role with consummate ease.

House of Flying Daggers is by turns romance, action and period epic, with Zhang Yimou beautifully blending digital trickery with the astounding kung fu sequences choreographed by Tony Ching. The result is a truly stunning spectacle. The way the daggers glide through the air in *Matrix*-style "bullet time" is no doubt cool, but it's the way that Zhang again uses colors to texture his scenes that sets the film apart: subtly bleeding the verdant bamboo greens into the golden red of autumn and finally, tragically, into the bleak white of winter.

In the Heat of the Sun
1995

Yangguang Canlan de Rizi

The Cultural Revolution – as a number of films in this book can testify – left a scar on China's collective psyche, and art helped the people to remember, criticize and condemn that period. But actor-turned-writer/director Jiang Wen's *In the Heat of the Sun*, which depicts 1970s China through the eyes of a teenage boy, is an anomaly. Jiang, in providing a voiceover about his mischievous youthful exploits, conveys a unique sense of longing for the era. It seems an odd choice to explore this period through a *Stand by Me*-esque coming of age film, but this adaptation of Wang Shuo's novel is more than that. The director uses ethereal visuals and sexuality (both figurative and literal) to compare this uncomfortable period in Chinese history to the awkward transition that is teenage sexual awakening.

The 15-year-old protagonist, Ma Xiaojun, is the badly behaved son of an army officer. Given his dad's absence, he receives little punishment from his mother and is free to do as he likes. He and most of his peers exhibit the same behavior at school; nobody stops them from misbehaving and others are especially hesitant to intervene in the fights of rival street gangs. Ma has a penchant for cracking locks, which he uses to break into homes, open his father's locked drawer (damaging a condom and facilitating the arrival of his baby sister in the process) and sneak into the room of the beautiful Mi Lan. Ma introduces her to his group, and demonstrates his street skills to her by climbing (a decidedly phallic) smoke stack and stalking over the roofs of the local *hutong* homes like a wild animal. Although Mi coquettishly

Director
Jiang Wen

Screenwriter
Jiang Wen

Cast
Jiang Wen
Xia Yu
Ning Jing
Tao Hong
Siqin Gaowa

Running time
134 minutes

陽光燦爛的日子
IN THE HEAT OF THE SUN
姜文第一回導演作品
改編自王朔原著小說"動物兇猛"

allows Ma to pour hot water over her head as she washes her
hair, her affections lie with the older members of the group.
The intra-gang rivalry comes to a head at Mi's birthday, when
Ma is beaten up by the older boys. Or is he? The voiceover
begins to question the accuracy of his memories, but what
is certain is that he splits from the group. This portion of the
film ends with the gang throwing Ma into the water and
repeatedly dunking his head in over and over again, a hint
that is as close as we get to the relentless violence of the
1970s.

Ma's longing for his colorful past is contrasted with a
black and white epilogue set in the present. Now grown-up,
Ma (played by Jiang) drives through Beijing in a limousine,
taking in the wholesale changes that have occurred, not just
to society, but to the very city around him. Jiang's film may
challenge the established view of the Cultural Revolution
– a fact which critics were quick to jump on – but it also adds
much-needed nuance to our interpretations of that difficult
period.

Bianlian

The King of Masks
1996

The King of Masks deals with two of the heavyweight issues gnawing away at contemporary Chinese society: preservation of a cultural legacy and shifting gender roles. This bittersweet effort from director Wu Tianming does much to highlight the conflict inherent between these issues. It is the story of an old artist whose inherited skill of "face changing" with Peking opera masks is in danger of being lost. However, when presented with an apparent heir to pass his tricks on to, he is hamstrung by his need for a boy. The higher value placed on male heirs, which has been exacerbated by the one child policy, may seem an antiquated view to some foreign audiences, but it still resonates with Chinese viewers. Tradition, the film tells us, is worth preserving, but outdated and irrational views are not.

Wang Bianlian (Zhu Xu) is aging, but he is still the finest "face changer" for miles around. His solitary life is spent begging for coins in town and sleeping on a boat with only his pet monkey for company. Many, including a local Peking opera star, want to learn Wang's secrets, but he is steadfast in his decision to only pass on this knowledge to a son. Old and single, his only recourse is to purchase a child in the local child market (yes, it's as horrific as it sounds), where he finds a reasonably priced young lad by the name of Gou Wa ("Doggie"). With newfound energy, Wang is able to concentrate on performing and begins to collect more substantial earnings from his act. Yet all is not what it seems, and when Wang discovers that Wa is a girl, he drives her away.

Director
Wu Tianming

Screenwriters
Wei Minglun

Cast
Zhu Xu
Zhou Renying
Zhao Zhigang

Running time
91 minutes

"You've got a little teapot spout! You really are heaven sent."

On her own, Gou Wa and a small boy are kidnapped by a gang of child-catchers. The boy, it later turns out, is from a rich family and a search for him begins with great intensity. The crafty Gou Wa manages to escape with him and they return to her master's boat. Believing that the living Buddha has answered his prayers, Wang takes the child in as his own. When the authorities discover the boy is in his care, however, Wang is arrested and sentenced to death. But fate is on Wang's side and Gou Wa leads a crusade to set him free and ultimately threatens to hangs herself during a public performance. The commanding officer is shamed into releasing Wang, who, recognizing Gou Wa's virtuous efforts, decides to teach her his secrets.

Stuffed to the brim with Confucian morality, filled with vivid cinematography and an exotic depiction of early 20th century China, *The King of Masks* was an international success. Wu Tianming had already established himself as a producer at the Xi'an Film Company – helping to launch the careers of Chen Kaige and Zhang Yimou – but with *The King of Masks*, he proved his own skill behind the camera.

Tianyunshan Chuanqi

The Legend of Tianyun Mountain
1980

As the dust began to settle on the Cultural Revolution, the film studios began to reopen. Those who managed to escape the "lost" decade relatively unscathed were ready to start making movies again. Director Xie Jin, whose films had been so popular and influential prior to 1964, was not about to forget the pain that so many Chinese people had endured. Xie became a proponent of the "scar" genre, a movement with roots in literature and the visual arts, which dealt with the pain, anger and resentment left over from the Mao era. Rather than criticizing the Cultural Revolution in general, *The Legend of Tianyun Mountain* targets the Anti-Rightist Campaign of the 1950s. As usual with Xie's films, the focus is on interpersonal relationships and events are told through the perspective of strong female characters.

The film begins as two recent graduates from college, Song Wei (Wang Fuli) and Feng Qinglan (Shi Jianlan), go on an expedition to Tianyu Mountain. While there, Song falls for Luo Qun (Shi Weijian), the newly appointed regional political leader, who convinces Song to join the Communist Party. They plan to get married, but Luo is declared a rightist and is fired from his post by Wu Yao, the leader of the Anti-Rightist Campaign in Tianyu Mountain. Under the strain of these events, Song breaks up with Luo and marries Wu. Feng, who has long harbored a secret love for Luo, leaves the Tianyu Expedition Company to find him exiled in a rural village. They are married and live a happy, if impoverished, existence. The film leaps forward 20 years to the fall of the Gang of Four. Wu is a senior official in the regional government and Song has

Director
Xie Jin

Screenwriter
Lu Yanzhou (novel)

Cast
Wang Fuli
Shi Jianlan
Shi Weijian
Zhong Xinghuo

Running time
120 minutes

an important role within the Communist Party. By chance, Song discovers that Luo still resides near Tianyu Mountain and is still labeled a rightist. Feeling guilty, Song sets out to rescue Luo from his pitiful fate. Wu tries to block her efforts, but Song goes above him in the Party and secures his pardon. For Feng, however, the news comes too late. After a lifetime of hardship, she succumbs to ill health and dies. In the film's telling final image, Song watches Luo from afar as he holds a silent vigil at Feng's grave.

Many Chinese emerged from the Mao years feeling strong resentment, and Xie Jin's remarkably bleak film channels that bitterness. It boldly criticizes the Party's injustices, showing how many good people were wrongly accused and severely punished. With *The Legend of Tianyun Mountain*, Xie rejected the filmmaking traditions that had come to define his socialist realism, employing devices such as voice over and flashback in a new manner. Xie was the last of the old guard, and his techniques would set the stage for the arrival of the "Fifth Generation."

Yi Ge Mosheng Nüren de Laixin

Letter from an Unknown Woman
2004

Cinephiles worth their salt should be familiar with this film's title, which comes from German auteur Max Ophüls' 1948 adaptation of a Stefan Zweig novella. Writer/director Xu Jinglei drew from the same source material for her adaptation, but moved the action to China. Originally, she intended to set the film between the 1970s and 1990s, but due to the films themes – prostitution and unmarried mothers – the more politically safe late 1940s were chosen. In many ways, Xu's film, despite inventing several characters, remains closer to Zweig's original than Ophüls' critically acclaimed version.

A renowned writer (played by Jiang Wen, perhaps the finest actor of his generation), receives the eponymous letter on his birthday. The letter opens: "My son died yesterday", and sets off a series of flashbacks, elaborating on a past relationship with a woman (played by Xu herself) who he had entirely forgotten. As he reads the words, the film's sumptuous cinematography brings the romance back to life. In their initial meeting, the woman, Jiang, was in her young teens and had a schoolgirl crush on her neighbor. The two meet again when Jiang returns to Beijing to study at university and a brief erotic encounter results in her pregnancy. Within a few days, though, the writer forgets it even happened.

Jiang retreats to Sichuan, which is in the throes of the Second World War, where gives birth to her son. When the war is over and the child is old enough, she returns to work as hostess in a Beijing club. The seedy profession is a

Director
Xu Jinglei

Screenwriter
Xu Jinglei

Cast
Xu Jinglei
Jiang Wen
Lin Yuan
Sun Feihu
Su Xiaoming

Running time
90 minutes

necessity if she is to provide for her son, of whom the writer is still unaware. The couple meets once more and though the writer senses something familiar about her, he is unable to actually remember who she is.

Xu's brave attempt to remake a well-established classic in China is admirable, exploring the ways in which people's self-worth can be greatly ignored by others. The film looks exquisite and instantly connected with audiences by giving voice to that indescribably painful feeling of loving someone who doesn't even know you exist.

Liang Shanbo yu Zhu Yingtai

Liang Shanbo and Zhu Yingtai
1954

Peking opera is one of those delicacies championed for unmatched brilliance by some, but bemoaned as insufferably tortuous by others. Either way, the role it has played in the evolution of Chinese cinema cannot be understated. This book would be incomplete without the inclusion of *Liang Shanbo and Zhu Yingtai*, one of the finest filmed examples of the art form ever committed to celluloid. You could classify the film as a musical in the very broadest sense of the term, but a better label would be *"guzhuang xi"* or "costume drama". This film and others in its genre were widely embraced in Mainland China until political realities halted production of such films. The genre continued to thrive for years in Taiwan and Hong Kong, where they were also popular.

The story is a gender-bending Buddhist retelling of *Romeo and Juliet* with a Peking opera twist. Zhu Yingtai is the daughter of a well-to-do family, who yearns for the chance to study at school, where only men are allowed to attend. She disguises herself as a man and travels to Hangzhou to begin her education, but *en route* she meets Liang Shanbo, developing an attachment that eventually blossoms into romantic love. The problem is that Liang is under the impression his new companion Zhu is…you know, a man. Her dalliance with education must come to an end and Zhu is forced to return home to her father, but not before coquettishly dropping hints to Liang as to her gender. Liang only realizes the truth after her departure and rushes after to gain her hand in marriage. The path for the star-crossed lovers is by no means smooth, and when Zhu arrives home,

Directors
Sang Hu
Hu Sha

Screenwriters
Xu Jin
Sang Hu

Cast
Yuan Xuefen
Fan Ruijuan
Zhang Guifeng

Running time
106 minutes

she discovers her father has already promised her to another man. Zhu and Liang are reunited, but their time is spent in utter sadness. Liang dies of heartbreak and Zhu, hearing the news on the way to her wedding, diverts her route to stop by Liang's tomb. As she mourns his death, an ominous cloud appears and lightning strikes the tomb, allowing Zhu to enter. As quickly as it opened, the tomb closes again and the pair, who have left this mortal world, are reincarnated as a pair of dancing butterflies.

Filmed performances often lack the visual flare of on-location shooting, so in order to record the intricate vocal performances and instruments, a soundstage was built for the film. Rich in color, the elegant costumes and playfulness of the performers render *Liang Shanbo and Zhu Yingtai* the most watchable addition to a genre that is for most an acquired taste.

Lin Jia Puzi

The Lin Family Shop
1959

Adapted from a story by famed novelist Mao Dun (then Minister of Culture in Chairman Mao's government), *The Lin Family Shop* is a damning portrait of the pre-Communist era. The film harkens back to earlier Chinese films like *The Goddess* and *Little Toys*, espousing simplistic Marxist theory with a dash of melodrama. As the tragedy unfolds, it's difficult to know who to sympathize with, but not what to blame: capitalism!

As the opening narration explains, the period before the Japanese invasion was the lowest time in China's history, truly dog-eat-dog. The film is set in a small town not far from Shanghai during the run up to the Spring Festival, when debts are traditionally repaid. Xie Tian stars as the patriarch of the Lin family and the decision maker in the family shop. Mr. Lin stocks a large variety of Japanese-made goods, the sale of which, after international tensions cause a wave of anti-Japanese sentiment, is halted by the local magistrate. After bribing the Kuomintang official and replacing the Japanese labels with Chinese ones, Mr. Lin continues to sell his contraband, even after full-out war has broken out with Japan. Soon, Lin's creditors come in search of the money they had lent him, but he is unable to pay. To save himself, he puts the squeeze on his workers and the farmers who rent his land. The cascading financial misfortunes mount (an interesting critique of capitalism's shortcomings) and when Mr. Lin is on the verge of bankruptcy, he skips town to avoid paying his debts, leaving his wife and daughter behind to face the music.

Director
Shui Hua

Screenwriters
Xia Yan
Mao Dun (novel)

Cast
Xie Tian
Lin Bin
Yu Lan
Chen Shou

Running time
83 minutes

"The big fish eat the small fish and the small fish eat the shrimp."

Director Shui Hua is a master of detail. Every cash transaction has a fetishistic quality about it – from the counting of coins to the rapid skill with which the characters use the abacus. Money, or more importantly the pursuit of it, is the root of all evil in this film. Shui does not demonize Mr. Lin, but sympathizes with his situation. Just as Lin wrongs the people below him, he is the victim of corrupt officials and untrustworthy businessmen above him. Xie Tian plays the part of Lin to perfection, helping us to understand his decisions even though we cannot completely approve of them. For Xie, this role was just another example of the great tragedy that marked his life. He could have had a prolific career, but external political pressures forced him to commit suicide.

Lin Zexu

Lin Zexu
1959

For the Chinese, the Opium Wars are a stain on their history. The trade disputes between the British Empire and Qing Dynasty, and the mass influx of opium into China rocked its society. But in tough times, heroes emerge – men like Lin Zexu. This biopic, despite its highly nationalistic tone, is among the most technically sophisticated Chinese films of the pre-Cultural Revolution era.

In the film, Lin Zexu is a high-ranking commissioner sent by Emperor Daoguang to Canton (modern day Guangzhou) to research the effects of the opium trade. Not wanting to arouse suspicion, Lin disguises himself as a merchant so that he can freely observe the sale of opium and the damage it inflicts on the local population. Lin discovers a group of foreigners dealing opium and demands they destroy their illicit bounty. When they refuse, Lin barricades them in their factory. One of the foreigners, with the aid of a corrupt official, flees the house, but is caught by a local fisherman. Hearing this news, Lin persuades the emperor that more coastal defenses are needed to protect the people from opium – a tactical necessity strengthened by a moral need. It's then that we meet Elliot, the British Ambassador to China, who promises that all the opium dealers will hand over their contraband and the Chinese government will be reimbursed for the damage caused. Of course those dastardly Brits have something else in mind. After Lin has burned all the opium, the British war ships begin to descend on Canton and the First Opium War begins. Shocked by what has happened, the Chinese emperor gives in to British demands, which

Directors
Zheng Junli
Qin Fan

Screenwriters
Lu Dang
Ye Yuan

Cast
Zhao Dan
Han Fei
Gao Bo
Qin Yi
Wen Xiying

Running time
99 minutes

include removing Lin from his position and the destruction of the coastal defenses. But whereas history painted a bleak ending for Lin, the movie ends on a more saccharine note: as Lin begins his journey into exile, an army of Chinese soldiers attack and kill a squadron of British troops.

The historical garb in the film is dazzling, especially when compared to the rather drab sartorial choices made in other Chinese films from the 1950s. With *Lin Zexu*, Zhang Junli and Qin Fan crafted an exquisite historical drama, rich in action and fulfilling the need to stoke patriotism during the Great Leap Forward.

Xiao Wanyi

Little Toys
1933

If ever there was a Chinese film made out of necessity, *Little Toys* is it. Like most movies made in the 1930s, it simply drips with political commentary. Many of the era's films, such as *The Goddess* and *Spring Silkworms*, were made by directors, producers and screenwriters with left-leaning tendencies – highly critical of the KMT regime. But *Little Toys* is a patriotic film aimed at strengthening the backbone of the average Chinese citizen, intensifying their feelings of national pride and their faith in government.

Ruan Lingyu was Chinese silent cinema's most famous star, and her role as Sister Ye was a defining moment of a short career in which she often played tragic characters that echoed her own off-screen misery. Before she committed suicide at age 25, she played a rape victim twice and took her own life four times on screen. She avoids these tragedies in *Little Toys*, but her fate is far from pleasant.

Sister Ye is a rural village's key toymaker, designing innovative products she and her fellow villagers can sell in the city. Her hapless husband – chided by the villagers for being fat and stupid – is charged with selling her wares. Double tragedy strikes when Ye's husband is killed by invading warlords and her son is taken by an opportunistic couple during the attack. Over the coming years, Ye and her daughter work valiantly in the face of "foreign toys", which are taking pride of place in the big cities over the quaint designs she and the fellow villagers produce. In need of money, Ye moves to Shanghai, but before long (wouldn't you know it) tragedy strikes again: her daughter, now grown, is killed by

Director
Sun Yu

Screenwriter
Sun Yu

Cast
Ruan Lingyu
Yuan Congmei
Li Lili
Luo Peng
Han Lan'gen

Running time
103 minutes

"Zhu'er, only idiots cry."

Japanese invaders. Ye becomes destitute, half-crazed and ridiculed, suffering until her final hours.

Although tragic, Sun Yu's film was actually seen as a moral lesson: just standing idly by will not protect you from the threat of invading economic, cultural and imperialist forces. The only way for China to get through this period of hardship was to strengthen its resolve in the face of hardships, and this film brought comfort to those who had already suffered.

Production company Lianhua had links with the KMT government, hence the film's slant, but they also championed a more visual style of film-making, rejecting the more dramatic acting techniques from Chinese theater. The end result here was a highly accomplished film that set itself apart from most everything else being made at the time.

Taitai Wan Sui

Long Live the Wife
1947

Given the historical context in which it was made, *Long Live the Wife* is a breath of fresh air. While most directors were unapologetically obsessed with revolutionary politics, Sang Hu instead looked at the power struggles of the household rather than the battlefield. Wenhua Film Studio was known for being more concerned with the quality of the pictures they produced than the message they were conveying. With a script penned by famed author Eileen Chang – whose short story *Lust, Caution* (1979) was made into an espionage thriller by Ang Lee in 2007 – the film helped start a wave of melodramas that remained popular for a number of decades in Taiwan.

Taken at face value, the film's plot is a little hard to fathom. Jiang Tianliu plays Chen Sizhen, a strong-willed woman who suffers her adulterous husband Tang Zhiyuan (Zhang Fa). Not only has Tang taken a mistress (Shangguan Yunzhu), but he also borrows money from Chen's father to fund his business ventures. Tang's mistress thinks she can easily manipulate him and gain the upper hand over his wife, but underestimates the resourcefulness of Chen, who is able to use her victim status to keep her husband under her thumb. Without ever wanting to disrupt the social order, Chen is able to win her husband back from the more glamorous woman who has taken him away. Although ostensibly the husband is the one in control, he is in fact at the mercy of two women, both aware of their sexuality and how to use it to get what they want. The dialog in the film snaps along with a real comedic edge. Eileen Chang drew

Director
Sang Hu

Screenwriter
Eileen Chang

Cast
Jiang Tianliu
Shi Hui
Zhang Fa
Shangguan Yunzhu

Running time
107 minutes

upon her own experiences in writing the screenplay – her mother and father divorced after the latter took a mistress – and this biting satire is a wonderful examination of the Chinese social order.

Subtle touches throughout the film hint at China's gender imbalance – Chen wears traditional Chinese-style clothing at home to suggest her dedication to her husband, but ventures out wearing European-style clothing almost as an act of defiance. Along with *Spring in a Small Town*, this film portrays a seemingly "powerful" male character as flawed and despicable. Chang's script is in some ways comparable to the American fast-talking comedies of the 1930s like *His Girl Friday*, but along with the good humor, she also demonstrates a great ability for biting social commentary in this very Chinese battle of the sexes.

Pingguo

Lost in Beijing
2007

Although the headlines surrounding Li Yu's banned film might lead you to believe it's only about sex, what really makes it relevant today is its brutal depiction of the collision between traditional Chinese values and the pressures brought about by China's economic miracle. True, Liu Pingguo (Fan Bingbing), a masseuse at the local Golden Basin Massage Parlor, and her window cleaning husband, An Kun (Tong Dawei), practice techniques "learned from a porno", but the amorous action is never titillating or in any way pleasant. Sex is used by the main characters as an act of possession, revenge, violence and despair, as they become entangled in – and the victims of – a sequence of increasingly devastating circumstances. The film's blunt portrayal of rape and violence towards women make it hard to watch at times, but the underlying social situations it exposes are of vital importance.

After drunkenly stumbling into work and passing out, Liu Pingguo is raped by her boss, Lin Dong. Lin is a hideous but successful Guangdong businessman with all the stereotypical accoutrements: flat-top, gold chains and man purse; played with alarming believability by Tony Leung Ka Fai. The attack is witnessed by An Kun as he cleans the windows. Distraught and seeking revenge, An tries to extort money from Lin's heavily made-up wife, Wang Mei (Elaine Jin), who, in a strange turn of events, ends up seducing him. Soon Liu discovers she is pregnant, but is unsure who the father is. On hearing the news, Lin and Wang – who had thought themselves infertile – decide that, if blood tests prove that Lin is the father, they will raise the child as their

Director
Li Yu

Screenwriters
Li Fang
Li Yu

Cast
Fan Bingbing
Tony Leung Ka Fai
Tong Dawei
Elaine Jin

Running time
112 minutes

own and pay the Liu and An a large sum of money for the privilege.

All of the central characters are *waidi* (Chinese from other regions), lured to Beijing in the hope of improving their lives. For Liu and An, keeping their heads above water is a day-to-day challenge, and for Lin and Wang the outward appearance of a normal family life, which a baby would provide, means everything. The Faustian pact the couples enter into stretches the bonds of all relationships to their breaking points; meanwhile, Liu Pingguo becomes a pawn in the others' power struggles.

For SARFT (State Administration of Radio Film and Television), *Lost in Beijing* presented an unrealistic and unhealthy view of Beijing to outsiders in the run up to the Olympics. The bureau thus revoked the film's Mainland screening license (effectively banning the film) in early 2007. Two versions of the film remain available online and on DVD: the full cut, which screened at the Berlin Film Festival, and a highly sanitized version (minus 20 minutes of sex, shots of Beijing monuments and anything remotely negative). Though the characters and their situations can border on hokey, the story is a remarkably brave effort from news-presenter-turned-director Li Yu. The film is shot and edited to give the impression of a dream-like daze, accentuating the idea that the characters are somehow lost in Beijing's urban haze. It uses broad, sometimes clumsy strokes to create an unflattering portrait of Beijing just before its Olympic "coming out", but the snapshot is valid and distressingly plausible.

Hei Jun Ma

A Mongolian Tale
1994

Zhang Chengzhi is a singular Chinese author. A Hui minority Muslim, he attended middle school at Tsinghua University and was a member of the first faction of youthful revolutionaries to use the moniker "Red Guard" during the Cultural Revolution. Inspired by the policy of sending students "up to the mountains and down to the villages", Zhang convinced 10 students to join him in extensively traveling around northwest China. During the four years he spent in Inner Mongolia, Zhang assimilated himself into the local culture, learned the local dialect and began to write poetry and fiction in this language. The experience was, on the whole, a positive one for Zhang, and when he reflected on it, he was filled with a nostalgia that few of his contemporaries felt for the era. This rose-tinted view that celebrates the simplicity of rural life permeates nearly every aspect of *A Mongolian Tale* – the screenplay of which Zhang adapted from his own novel.

The story opens on the verdant Mongolian steppe, where Nai Nai – played by veteran actress Dalarsurong – toils as a shepherd to provide for herself and her orphaned granddaughter, Someyer. Despite the rigors of their nomadic existence, Nai Nai willingly opens her door (well, the flaps of her yurt) to a young motherless boy whose father is unable to look after him. Nai Nai names the boy Bayinbulag and raises him as Someyer's brother. The family gets by happily, but in poverty. They are unable to afford a horse, but when a lost foal stumbles upon them, they take charge and it becomes Bayinbulag's. After receiving a basic education,

Director
Xie Fei

Screenwriter
Zhang Chengzhi

Cast
Tengger
Naranhua
Dalarsurong

Running time
103 minutes

Bayinbulag receives a letter from his father, saying that he must go to the city to study veterinary medicine. Upon leaving, he tells Someyer that he intends to come back and marry her in three years. When he returns, however, he finds that his would-be bride has become pregnant by another man.

Rocked by this revelation, Bayinbulag leaves and becomes a successful folk singer (Bayinbulag is played by Tingger, a real-life Mongolian pop-star, who contributed to the soundtrack), while Someyer marries her suitor and bears him three more children. When they meet again after 14 years have passed, the awkward interactions between Bayinbulag and Someyer's youngest daughter hint at the couple's lost opportunity.

Gorgeously shot, the film's greatest asset is its simple yet authentic touches of rural life in Inner Mongolia that make it one of the most eye-catching of China's ethnic minority film genre.

Mulan Congjun

Mulan Joins the Army
1939

Directors
Bu Wancang

Screenwriter
Ouyang Yuqian

Cast
Chen Yunshang
Mei Xi
Liu Jiqun
Huang Naishuang
Han Lan'gen

Running time
89 minutes

In the 1930s, Shanghai benefited from its "island" status. While the cities around it were succumbing to Japanese control, Shanghai's foreign concessions – largely controlled by the British, Americans and French – became a sanctuary for creative freedom. Naturally, such artistic license was embraced by groups of patriotic Chinese intellectuals, who were able to imbue their cinematic efforts with strong nationalistic themes, usually concealed in a historical framework. The Wan brothers attempted this with their animated adventures (see *Princess Iron Fan* and *Havoc in Heaven*), but it was Bu Wancang's *Mulan Joins the Army* that was most successful at sneaking a message of national unity under the noses of the Japanese.

Ouyang's script remains reasonably faithful to the Mulan myth as well as the widely performed Peking opera. *Mulan Joins the Army* is set during the Northern Dynasties period (386-581 AD), a time when tribes from Mongolia and northern China began to invade the south. Hua Mulan is an avid practitioner of martial arts, which she learned from her old warhorse of a father. When the government urges Mulan's father to take up arms, he realizes his maiming days are behind him and Mulan disguises herself as a man to go in his place. It's not long before her fellow soldiers recognize her ability and brains, and Mulan is promoted to sergeant and later, when her predecessor is wounded, general. Under her guidance, a counterattack is launched, driving the enemy into retreat. During the battle, however, Mulan's best friend and comrade, Liu, discovers the truth about her gender, but

helps keep it a secret. Mulan and Liu are greatly rewarded by the emperor with promotions. But instead of enjoying the fruits of their arduous toil, they decide to look after those in need: Mulan turns to her ageing parents and Liu looks after the injured general. With the war behind them, Mulan assumes her female identity once more and marries Liu.

Based on the legend of Hua Mulan, the story would have been firmly embedded in the nation's consciousness; but, whereas the traditional story was a comment on the importance of filial piety, screenwriter Ouyang Yuqian includes a subtle but prominent message of the need for national solidarity. Most of Shanghai's established stars had either fled to Hong Kong or Chongqing after the Japanese occupation, so Nancy Chan (Chen Yunshang) was recruited from Hong Kong. In this Shanghainese production she proved her versatility, simultaneously recording the film in Cantonese and Mandarin to allow distribution in both territories.

Chengnan Jiushi

My Memories of Old Beijing
1983

The indelicate transition from the wide-eyed innocence of childhood to the harsh realities of adulthood has been well explored as a subject in literature, film and other artistic mediums. Wu Yigong's adaptation of the novel *My Memories of Old Beijing* by Lin Haiyin, however, breathes fresh life into the age-old theme.

When the six-year-old Yingzi arrives in the capital in the 1920s, she is captivated by her surroundings: the Great Wall, the camel caravans and the narrow *hutongs*, full of potential friends. The first person to make an impression on her is Xiuzhen, a woman whose erratic behavior is hard for the young girl to understand. Xiuzhen has been left utterly devastated by the loss of her child, Xiao Guizi. She wanders the streets mumbling the girl's name and is consumed with the thought of rediscovering her. Xiuzhen's husband is also missing, taken away by the police several years ago with no explanation. Thoughtful and intuitive, Yingzi locates a child living nearby named Xiao Guizi, who bears the missing girl's characteristic mole on the back of her neck. A blissful reunion ensues, but is short-lived. Xiuzhen goes off in search of her husband to complete the family unit, but she and Xiao Guizi are struck by a train and die. Yingzi is heart-broken, but soon befriends a young man who steals in order to pay for his brother's education. He is similarly cursed by Yingzi's friendship, as she accidentally gives the location of his secret hiding place to a policeman and he is arrested.

Her feelings about the city begin to change as the seasons pass and we next find Yingzi at the age of nine. At

Director
Wu Yigong

Screenwriter
Yi Ming

Cast
Shen Jie
Zheng Zhenyao
Zhang Fengyi
Zhang Min

Running time
96 minutes

this point she is closest to her nanny, Song, a hardworking woman who looks after all of Yingzi's needs. Yingzi wonders why Song would look after someone else's family if she has one of her own. We later learn that Song's son tragically drowned and her daughter was sold off by her husband. Performing menial tasks for another family is her only way of providing for herself and her husband. The film's final drama affects Yingzi more directly: her father contracts lung cancer and dies, forcing Yingzi and her mother to relocate away from Beijing. The city of her childhood dealt her many harsh lessons about the realities of adult life and, as she looks back on it as an old woman, tears cascade down her face.

The film is not about a sexual awakening, but rather the moment when we realize that life is not as happy and carefree as we would like. For Yingzi, this awareness comes through the harrowing events that befall those around her. With lyrical structure, plot development and settings that parallel China's own fragmented development, *My Memories of Old Beijing* is a loss-of-innocence tale with distinctly Chinese elements.

Wanjia Denghuo

Myriad of Lights
1948

Like many films in the 1930s and '40s, *Myriad of Lights* sought to strip away Shanghai's dazzling façade and portray the hardships that ordinary Chinese living there were facing. It also explores the time-honored town-versus-country conflict where, due to its left-leaning politics, the country folk are represented as honest and hardworking, much preferable to the corrupt and morally bankrupt city dwellers. Shangguan Yunzhu stars as Lan Youyan, an impoverished family matriarch. Shangguan was a well-known actress in her day, but it's her personal life that she is best known for now. Shortly before the beginning of the Cultural Revolution she had a brief affair with Chairman Mao, a fact that ultimately led to her persecution in the coming years and eventual suicide.

Hu Zhiqing is a simple man who struggles in Shanghai to provide for his wife Lan Youyan and his daughter. His office worker's wage is stretched further when his mother and his brother's family move from the provinces to live with him under the mistaken belief that things will be easier in the big city (although he still keeps a servant). Life goes from bad to worse for Hu, as his apartment becomes cramped and his meager salary is not enough to support his family, especially not with his wife expecting another child. His boss deals him another blow, firing him after a disagreement over how to run the business. The resulting stress causes Youyan to have a miscarriage, and things (as if they weren't already bad) become unbearable as Hu is mistaken for a pickpocket, beaten and, shortly afterwards, run over. Taken to a hospital,

Director
Shen Fu

Screenwriters
Shen Fu
Yang Hansheng

Cast
Lan Ma
Shangguan Yunzhu
Wu Yin
Shen Yang
Gao Zheng

Running time
121 minutes

he remains in a coma for several days and after recovering returns home to find his whole extended family gathered, promising to face their troubles together.

Such a rapid succession of mishaps almost appears farcical, but it's typical of the cinema of the period. Audiences appreciated tales of suffering and misfortune, which echoed the terrible living conditions they themselves were experiencing. Cinema was not seen as a place to escape from reality, but rather a venue where, through the suffering of others, some sort of catharsis could be achieved.

Jiawu Fengyun

Naval Battle of 1894
1962

The 1950s was a decade characterized in Mainland China by the clumsy integration of cinema and politics. After some impressive (and not-so-impressive) films, Chinese directors hit their stride in the 1960s, producing pictures that satisfied both the Party and the audience. The aesthetic of 1960s' films was firmly rooted in socialist realism, the cinematic style that would dominate Chinese moviemaking until the 1980s.

Like most of director Lin Nong's more successful films, *Naval Battle of 1894* uses historic events to convey a contemporary political message. This technique would not always serve him well; his films often caught the attention of high-ranking party officials. Zhou Enlai had to personally approve Lin's film *The Besieged City*. After incorporating suggested revisions, the Lin thought he would be immune from reprisals, but political in-fighting during the Cultural Revolution led to the film being banned by Zhou's enemies.

Naval Battle of 1984 concerns the lead up to the first Sino-Japanese War in 1894, as prime minister Li Hongzhang refuses to allow commander of the Chinese North Sea Fleet Ding Ruchang to patrol a route used by Chinese shipping firms. As a result, two cargo ships are sunk along with one of their two escorts. Aboard the surviving ship, captain Fang Boqian orders his crew to fly the white flag and retreat. But the crew takes matters into its own hands and counter-attacks, significantly damaging the Japanese ship and allowing for escape. The cowardly Fang is proclaimed a hero and takes the undue credit. When the commander of learns that Fang is not what he claims to be, he petitions to

Director
Lin Nong

Screenwriter
Xi Nong

Cast
Li Moran
Wang Qiuying
Pu Ke
Zhou Wenbin
Pang Xueqin

Running time
95 minutes

prove that the sailors, not their captain, deserve the praise. Arriving in Tianjin, Ding discovers the prime minister in negotiations with Allied Forces over how to deal with Japan. Secretly listening in, Ding hears the foreigners suggest a tactic of appeasement against the Japanese. When finally given court, Ding is incandescent with rage, lashing out at the hypocrisy of the foreign diplomats. For this affront to the prime minister, Ding is fired and only reinstated after the Chinese reluctantly declare war on the Japanese.

Ding's attacks on the Japanese ships are successful and his crew heavily damages the Japanese flagship, but they exhaust their ammunition. In a final battle cry, Ding orders his crew to ram the Japanese ship, kamikaze-style. But alas, they are torpedoed into oblivion before reaching their target.

The nationalistic message is obvious, but Lin Nong's excellent staging of the battles separates this from more run-of-the-mill propaganda. This of one of the easiest films of its era to enjoy without getting bogged down by the politics.

Zhufu

New Year's Sacrifice
1956

Seconds after the Beijing Film Studio logo fades away at the beginning of *New Year's Sacrifice*, we're presented with a bronze plaque featuring the venerable face of Lu Xun, the author of the short story upon which the film is based. This small gesture signifies two things: first, that literary adaptation had become so commonplace that films had developed their own corresponding visual conventions. Second, that whereas early Chinese films looked to the theater (operas and shadow puppets) for inspiration, the written word was now becoming the go-to source for inspiration.

Lu Xun is often regarded as the founder of modern Chinese literature, with Chairman Mao (a friend of the author's brother) being one of his greatest admirers. The difficult duty of adapting Lu's short story was left to Xia Yan, himself one of the most accomplished screenwriters and critics of his generation. At the helm was director Sang Hu, skilled at working with literary sources as in *Long Live the Wife* and *Phony Phoenixes*. With this much talent and the luxury of color film, it's no wonder *New Year's Sacrifice* was a huge success.

At its core, the film explores the role of women in traditional Chinese society and the pitiful fates that can befall them. A recently widowed woman overhears her mother-in-law plotting to sell her into an arranged marriage with another man. Rather than face a potentially loveless marriage, the widow flees her small town and gets a job as a maid in a wealthy residence far away. While laying the

Director
Sang Hu

Screenwriter
Xia Yan

Cast
Bai Yang
Wei Heling
Li Jingpo

Running time
100 minutes

126

foundations for a new life, she is kidnapped by a group of men hired by her mother-in-law to force her to go through with the marriage. She is betrothed to a farmer by the name of He Laoliu. He is an honest man, but he cannot convince the widow that a union would be to her benefit and she attempts to take her own life. His tenderness breaks down her feelings of animosity; they establish a normal marriage and have a baby boy. But good fortune is fleeting in Chinese movies. He dies of exhaustion and their child is killed by a wolf. Without a source of income, the house is repossessed by the landlord and the widow is forced to return to a life of servitude for the wealthy household. The descent does not end there. Her employers are sympathetic, but soon become frustrated with her repetitive stories and fire her. From there, she becomes a beggar, collapsing dead on the street on New Year's Eve. Some gift.

Lao Jing

Old Well
1987

Wu Tianming – director, actor and studio bigwig – had a hand in some of the most influential and successful Chinese movies of all time. As head of Xi'an Studios at the beginning of the 1980s, he helped bring the Fifth Generation into existence by supplying the finances necessary to make their ideas a reality. In 1987, in the directorial chair, he cast a 36-year-old cinematographer favored by Chen Kaige and Zhang Junzhao to star in his latest movie. With a face like a cracked jug (no doubt accentuated by chain-smoking), Zhang Yimou is not your typical leading man, but a year before he made his own directorial debut with *Red Sorghum*, he held his own as a man leading a village's desperate search for water.

The ironically named village of Laojing ("Old Well") is desperately short of water and opportunities: only three inhabitants have received a high school-level education. Sun Wangquan (Zhang Yimou) is one of the bright young things and the latest hope in a long line of villagers desperate to find a viable water source. The dedication required to obtain the elusive substance has forced Sun to subjugate all other aspects of his life. His high school sweetheart, Qiaoying, must be spurned so that Sun can marry a local widow capable of providing a sizable dowry. When he attempts to flee the village with Qiaoying, his meddling grandfather ensures his return to marry the "correct" woman.

Sun is sent into the nearest town to learn the engineering basics needed in his quest for water. When he returns, he and Qiaoying lead an underground expedition. The claustrophobic and ultimately dangerous search traps

Director
Wu Tianming

Screenwriter
Zheng Yi

Cast
Zhang Yimou
Liang Yujin
Lu Liping

Running time
130 minutes

them underground with little hope of escape. Their life in the balance, Sun and Qiaoying confess their secret love... shortly before being rescued. One in their party, however, fares poorly and dies during the search.

Finally, when a potential well is located, the only barrier to a clean supply of water is financial. To secure the required funds, all the villagers make sacrifices: Sun's grandfather donates his coffin and Qiaoying, soon to be married, gives up her wedding gifts to raise the cash necessary to secure the *aqua vita*. The villagers tenacity and "kitchen sink" approach, abandoning everything in search of development, is a sly look at China's march towards modernity and the often overlooked human costs.

129

一个和八个

Yi Ge he Ba Ge

One and Eight
1983

Yellow Earth takes all the recognition as *the film* of the Fifth Generation of Chinese filmmakers, but *One and Eight* – made a year earlier and featuring the work of many of the 1982 Beijing Film Academy graduating class – was where it all started. Based on a narrative poem by Guo Xiaochuan, the film was a collaboration between Zhang Junzhao (director), Zhang Yimou (cinematographer) and He Qun (art designer). Together, they succeeded in bringing a vital new type of war movie to Chinese screens. As we would now expect, the film was heavily censored by the authorities for portraying criminals and other traitors to Communist principles as capable of heroism.

Similar to Robert Aldrich's *The Dirty Dozen* (1967) – in this case eight – the film is about a chain-gang making their way across the country while they await trial by the Chinese government during the Second Sino-Japanese War. The group is comprised of three deserters, three bandits, a Japanese spy, a landlord (the disreputable eight) and Wang Jin (the "one"), a wrongly accused Communist officer. As well as the group of convicts and soldiers, there is also a compassionate nurse, who treats the men tenderly. The majority of the Communist soldiers feel no sympathy whatsoever, refusing to believe any of Wang Jin's protestations of innocence. During the journey, the group comes under attack from the Japanese, and the Communist army loses its way. Right before the prisoners are about to be executed, it becomes necessary for the chain-gang to join the battle. Most fight heroically but are killed. The film

Director
Zhang Juzhao

Screenwriters
Wang Jicheng
Zhang Ziliang
Guo Xiaochuan

Cast
Tao Zeru
Chen Daoming
Lu Xiaoyan
Xie Yuan

Running Time
86 minutes

"The Chinese people wrote this epic with their flesh and blood."

ends with an iconic shot of a wounded Wang Jin carrying an injured soldier on his shoulders through a ravaged and desolate desert.

The film owes a great deal to the cinematography of Zhang Yimou – a converted photographer – whose breathtaking images in some scenes resemble woodblock prints. Although Zhang Juzhao never replicated this success with other films, with *One and Eight* he produced an original work that rejected the outdated techniques that were still being used by older generations. The version of the film available today is far from the intended result. It took two years, some 70 cuts, and some entirely reshot scenes before it was granted permission for release. Changes included those made to the final scene in which, to prevent her rape by a Japanese soldier, one of the bandits shoots the nurse. In the edited version, he saves her at the cost of his own life. The film is, however, still dramatic, visceral and bold, and for some viewers it will serve as a more palatable introduction to the Fifth Generation's ascendency than *Yellow Earth*.

GUANGXI FILM STUDIO

The 1982 graduating class of the Beijing Film Academy had the desire and talent to revolutionize Chinese cinema, but they needed the help of the Guangxi Film Studio (which produced both Yellow Earth *and* One and Eight*) to bring it about. Realizing the potential talent pool they could draw on, the Nanning-based production company offered more freedom and greater opportunities for young directors than Beijing or Shanghai studios. Their results were spectacular.*

131

San Mao Liulang Ji

An Orphan on the Streets
1949

A cursory glance through the history of Chinese cinema will show that hardly any films before 1950 were made specifically with children in mind. Any film that was in some way designed for children would usually cross over into comedy or fantasy. Therefore, *An Orphan on the Streets*, with its rambunctious protagonist and a story adapted from a series of comics by Zhang Leping, is all the more inviting.

San Mao (literally "three hairs") is an orphan child with three thick dreads of hair hanging from his head. His pangs of hunger are difficult for him to take and, after trippy visions of food flash before his eyes, he sets off to steal grub with other street urchins. While in the act, a recruiter for a street gang spots him and attempts to lure him into their operation. He might be destitute, but San Mao has principles, and he prefers instead to make a bit of extra cash by shining shoes, scavenging for rubbish and selling newspapers. But even his good intentions are seldom rewarded: he finds a wallet on the street and returns it to the owner, only to be beaten for suspicion of having pinched it. Fed up with life on the street, San Mao comes up with the ingenious idea of selling himself. With a cardboard sign around his neck, he sets off down the street, attracting the attention of a wealthy childless lady, who immediately adopts him and takes him to her home. A Little Orphan Annie style makeover ensues, where San Mao is bathed and dressed in a finely tailored Western suit and given the English name "Tom" to boot. The new sartorial style does not go well with San Mao's personality and he begins to resent the rigidity of his new lifestyle. His feelings

Director
Zhao Ming

Screenwriter
Yang Hansheng

Cast
Wang Longji
Guan Hongda
Wang Gongxu

Running time
71 minutes

of discomfort are exacerbated when, at a party thrown for him, he is greeted with a kiss from a little girl, who leaves a lipstick smudge on his cheek. Not one for creature comforts, San Mao throws off his symbolic clothes and runs away from the mansion to join his fellow urchins on the street. The finale sees the victorious People's Liberation Army marching into town, cheered by San Mao and his buddies as they arrive.

It's hard not to see San Mao as the Chinese answer to *The Little Rascals*. His escapades unfold with a tragicomic air that appealed to children as well as their parents, who no doubt enjoyed the criticisms of the Kuomintang government as told through a child's eyes. As for San Mao, the comic creature proved an enduring one, spawning many remakes and subsequent adventures including everything from *San Mao Runs a Business* (1958) to *San Mao Joins the Army* (1992), showing there are some universal film formulas that audiences just can't get enough of.

Xiao Wu

Pickpocket
1997

When the films of the Fifth Generation of Chinese directors made waves abroad in the early 1990s, their success inspired confidence within the usually conservative Beijing Film Academy, where a young film theory student, Jia Zhangke, was studying. By the time Jia graduated, however, he had become disillusioned with the flashy styles of Chen Kaige, Zhang Yimou and Tian Zhuangzhuang, who preferred to capture China's exotic past rather than its ever-changing present. Jia decided to make his first feature during a visit back to his hometown of Fenyang in Shanxi Province. Fenyang was a backwards place when Jia left for Beijing, but upon his return, he found that modernization efforts had transformed the city entirely.

Called *Pickpocket* in English – an indiscreet nod to French auteur Robert Bresson's film – the film stars Wang Hongwei as its anti-hero, struggling to stay afloat in a sea of flux. A petty thief, Xiao Wu is constantly evading the local law. His former partner has gone "legitimate", graduating into cigarette smuggling, and wants nothing to do with Xiao Wu. Melancholy and aimless, Xiao Wu cuts a dejected figure, crooning out of tune alone in one of the new KTV bars. He meets a KTV "comfort girl" (essentially a prostitute), Mei Mei (Hao Hongjian), and life seems to be improving. But everything in Fenyang is fleeting, and she disappears without a goodbye. Xiao Wu returns home and realizes his parents' relationship has become strained. Family is of the upmost importance in Chinese culture, but we learn that even it is not immune from ever-shifting Chinese social forces.

Director
Jia Zhangke

Screenwriter
Jia Zhangke

Cinematographer
Nelson Yu Lik-wai

Editor
Xiao Lingyu

Cast
Wang Hongwei
Hao Hongjian
Zuo Baitao
Ma Jinrei
Liu Junying

Running time
108 minutes

Jia Zhangke has said his movies are all about capturing the realities of Chinese life. For foreign audiences only familiar with the stylized visions of Chinese life in Chen Kaige's *Farewell My Concubine* or Bernardo Bertolucci's *The Last Emperor*, the realities of urban life presented in Jia's work can be quite shocking. Jia is a master of capturing the sights and, most particularly, the sounds of Fenyang. With background noise punctuating practically every scene – be it road construction, Mando-pop blaring out of a radio or a Hong Kong action flick on TV – silence is never achieved. At the film's core is a seemingly effortless performance by Wang Hongwei. At turns pathetic and miserable, he is someone you cannot help but feel sympathy for. He's a man completely unprepared to survive in the new world that has materialized around him; and it's these figures in China's recent history – the casualties of modernization – that Jia has chosen to follow throughout his glittering career.

Platform
2000

Zhantai

Small-town China can be a desolate place. At least, that's what you might gather from the films of Jia Zhangke. In his first feature-length film, *Pickpocket*, he presented his hometown, Fenyang, Shanxi Province, through the eyes of a lowly pickpocket. The grubby town and its people are shown as good-natured but overwhelmed by the pace of development. With *Platform*, Jia uses slightly more polished *mise-en-scène* to capture the dusty realism of *Pickpocket*. The authenticity is not altogether lost, as mixed in among the professional actors are a number of locals giving more natural performances. Whereas *Pickpocket* was set in contemporary China, in *Platform* Jia delved further back in time to discuss the rapid changes of China's past 30 years through theater.

Jia's regular collaborator, Wang Hongwei, plays Cui Minliang, who works with his friends in a traveling theatrical company based out of Fenyang. The year is 1979 and specter of the Cultural Revolution can still be seen in their dress (blue Zhongshan/Mao suits) and their choice of performances (socialist melodramas). Although rural and backwards, the tiny villages they tour are starting to see an influx of outside popular culture. In a stray piece of Western fashion or an up-tempo Taiwanese song, we see things slowly starting to change. With Deng Xiaoping in power, a new era begins and small additions are added to the company's repertoire, like the sultry flamenco dancing of Cui's girlfriend, Yin Ruijian (Zhao Tao). In 1984, the troupe is privatized by a new owner, Song Yongping, who brings with him hopes of a brighter

Director
Jia Zhangke

Screenwriter
Jia Zhangke

Cast
Wang Hongwei
Zhao Tao
Liang Jingdong

Running time
155 minutes

136

future. Yin is less enthusiastic about the new path the group intends to take and stays behind on their next tour. She settles for a boring but steady job as a tax collector, while the company undergoes a rapid transformation – gone are the revolutionary slogans, replaced by spandex, cheesy pop music and one of the kitschiest names imaginable, "All-Star Rock and Breakdance Electronic Band".

The subtle disappointment that the film conveys is stretched out over a viewer-testing 155 minutes, but Jia's patience is exemplary. He lets the story, characters and scenes develop organically, never rushing in his quest to capture something unique. Added here are touches of the absurd and a gentle sense of humor that he was criticized for lacking in his first film. This film is a deeply personal and pessimistic reflection on those hopeful early years of China's opening up, and the people who were left behind in the transition.

Nashan Naren Nagou

Postmen in the Mountains
1999

Postmen in the Mountains redefines "snail mail". The treacherous 122km round-trip journey to deliver the mail to mountainous villages in Hunan province takes the local postman (Teng Rujun) three days to complete. As he enters his 40s, his deteriorating health renders him unable to continue with his beloved position and he passes on the family occupation to his son (Liu Ye). The evening before his son sets off, the postman systematically packs up the letters, protecting them from any adverse weather. But when it's time for the son to leave, the boy's fretful mother complains and his father's trusted canine companion is unwilling to follow him. The father must therefore retrace the well-trod route one last time to teach his son.

The time they spend together on the journey is difficult. The nature of the job has kept them apart for long periods of time, so much so that the word "father" comes uneasily out of the son's mouth. Although the father wants to speak with his son, all that he can talk about as they trek through some of China's most beautiful surroundings is the job. The role of a postman is not simply to deliver letters, he explains, but also to act as a go-between, the conduit between these remote areas and the outside world. In one charming scene, the postman explains the plight of a blind woman. Her son regularly sends money, but the envelopes contain no messages or news. Each time he visits, the postman stages a "reading", inventing fictitious news from the son. Gradually, his own son begins to develop a solemn respect for his father's job and, through encounters with the grateful

Director
Huo Jianqi

Screenwriter
Si Wu

Cast
Ten Rujun
Liu Ye

Running time
111 minutes

那山那人那狗

POSTMAN IN THE MOUNTAINS

深山中，老邮差送了一辈子的信，
这一次，他不仅是送邮袋里的信，
还有父子传承教教那感情，
一个自然真实，扣人心弦的山中传奇……

荣 获
第十九届中国电影金鸡奖"最佳故事片" "最佳男主角"
加拿大蒙特利尔电影节"最受观众欢迎影片"
北京大学学生电影节"最佳男主角"

recipients of letters, he begins to understand this man who
has been absent from so much of his life.

Director Huo Jianqi and his longtime screenwriter/
wife weave subtle details about the nature of human
communication into their adaptation of Peng Jianming's
short story, but the little vignettes and the spectacular
natural scenery of Suining and Dao counties in southwestern
Hunan do most of the hard work. The film is as much about
the problems of communication between father and son
as respecting Confucian values. *Postmen in the Mountains'*
simple and poetic storytelling will strike a chord with even
the most cynical viewers.

Tie Shan Gongzhu

Princess Iron Fan
1941

Directors
Wan Guchan
Wan Laiming

Screenwriters
Wan Guchan
Wan Laiming

Cast
Bai Hong (voice)
Yan Yueling (voice)
Jiang Ming (voice)
Han Langen (voice)
Yin Xiuc (voice)

Running time
73 minutes

In 1939, Walt Disney's *Snow White and the Seven Dwarfs* (1937) finally made it across to the majority of China's eastern coastal cities where, after watching a screening in Shanghai, four brothers from Nanjing were inspired. Wan Laiming, along with his twin, Guchan, and younger brothers, Chaochen and Dihuan, had already produced China's first cartoon short, *Turmoil in the Workshop* (1926), influenced by the American cartoons of the 1920s. But with *Snow White*, the brothers were finally convinced that a feature-length cartoon could be used to bring to the big screen the most fantastical elements of one of China's most cherished stories: *Journey to the West*.

Endlessly adapted for the stage and screen, *Journey to the West* is the story of the monk Xuanzang and his helpers (a monkey, a pig and a horse) as they travel west to India to obtain important Buddhist texts. Such is the original book's length, over 100 chapters, that the Wan brothers decided to focus on one story, in which Xuanzang attempts to use an enchanted fan to put out the flames of the Fiery Mountain blocking his path. The Wan brothers had somewhat crude black and white animation skills, but produced something that must have appeared vivid and captivating to audiences in 1941. For the first time they could see larger-than-life, realistic representations of the fearsome Fiery Mountain and the impish Monkey King they knew so well. The film is highly evocative of the Disney style, but the Wan brothers were careful to retain as much Chinese artistic influence as possible in telling their story. Although not as polished as its

American counterparts, the film singled out the brothers as leaders in Chinese animation for decades to come.

Actually producing the film was a feat equal to those achieved by the cartoon characters it depicts: it was animated over a period of 16 months in a tiny studio in Shanghai's French Concession, partially under the control of the Vichy Government. The film is not immune to the political circumstances in which it was crafted, and the brothers inserted an important political message for the Chinese people: just as Xuanzang and his followers come together to defeat Princess Iron Fan, so must the Chinese people come together in order to overcome the Japanese occupation. The Japanese would eventually leave Shanghai in 1945, but they took *Princess Iron Fan* with them. The film was a big box office success in Japan and went on to influence many of the key animators for whom the country would become famous.

Raise the Red Lantern
1991

Da Hong Denglong
Gaogao Gua

Director
Zhang Yimou

Screenwriter
Ni Zhen

Cast
Gong Li
Ma Jingwu
He Saifei
Cao Cuifeng
Jin Shuyuan

Running time
124 minutes

Although not instantly apparent, Zhang Yimou's *Raise the Red Lantern* is an angry reaction to the violent repression of the Tian'anmen Square demonstrations in June 1989. But rather than laying specific blame, Zhang's film is a broad look at the underlying qualities that make up the Chinese national character. On the surface, the film attacks the old family system, as represented by Master Chen (Ma Jingwu) and his veracious appetite for concubines. His ritualistic approach to life and demands for subservience are seen to have a great capacity to erode individualism. For Zhang – like other young men sent to the countryside during the Cultural Revolution – daily rituals were once an important a part of life. Checking in with superiors and pledging allegiance to Chairman Mao were just some of the many dehumanizing aspects of that dark chapter in Chinese history.

After her father dies and leaves her mother penniless, Song Lian (Gong Li), a 19-year-old college student, agrees to become the fourth concubine of a rich patriarch. Although the marriage provides financial security for her mother, Song enters a world of solitude and servitude. Between Master Chen's concubines, a daily battle is fought to see with whom he will spend the night – the "chosen" woman is notified by having a red lantern lit above her quarters. Chen's first wife has virtually given up trying to entice him, due to her age and the fact that she has already borne him a male heir. Through her, Song learns that capturing Master Chen's affections and giving him a son will lead to greater freedom in the oppressive house. She fakes a pregnancy to please him, but her ruse is exposed by a jealous maid, and soon the red lantern appears less and less often outside her room. Her own lanterns are finally covered forever with black hoods. Song's fate, however, is better than that of Meishan – Chen's third mistress. Caught having an affair with the household doctor by the second mistress, Meishan is gagged, bound, taken to a room at the top of the compound and hanged. Song confronts the murderers, who show no remorse, and the event sets her on a descent into madness. The film culminates as a fifth mistress arrives at the compound, beginning the oppressive cycle anew.

Based on the novel by Su Tong, Zhang took significant liberties in moving the setting from China's damp and mildewy south to the dry and cold north. Zhang felt more comfortable shooting the architecture he was used to, and that familiarity helps to create a sense of imprisonment and an almost tangible sense of competition between the women, who are almost entirely subjugated to their master's will.

Du Jiang Zhencha Ji

Reconnaissance across the Yangtze
1954

While many of the films glorifying the Communist Revolution get bogged down in jingoistic rhetoric, *Reconnaissance across the Yangtze* provides instead a healthy dollop of action. The men and women of the Communist forces are portrayed as straight-backed, square-jawed and willing to give almost anything for the cause – characters from the socialist realist art of the time made flesh. Screen idol Sun Daolin exemplifies this and shows his versatility as an actor in role of the brave, upstanding General Li, a far cry from the timid but honest schoolteacher he portrays in *Crows and Sparrows*.

As the film's title suggests, this sleekly shot war movie is about a reconnaissance team of the People's Liberation Army sent to swim across the Yangtze River to investigate a Nationalist stronghold off of its northern banks. Li's crack team makes its way across the river at night and establishes contact with Sister Liu, the leader of a guerilla outfit. Once on the ground, they disguise themselves as peasants and Nationalist troops to avoid detection by the patrolling forces. The team steals vital tactical documents that highlight the weaknesses of the base; however, they are soon discovered by the Nationalists and are picked off one by one trying to keep hold of the data. Eventually, one member manages to get back across the river and give the information to the PLA, who unleash a coordinated attack on the Nationalist base. Thanks to the heroic efforts of Li's men, the attack is a complete success, but it is soon time for them to move on. Li bids goodbye to Sister Liu and his team moves south to look for other battles.

Director
Tang Xiaodan

Screenwriter
Shen Mojun

Cast
Sun Daolin
Qi Heng
Kang Tai
Chen Shu
Li Lingjun
Zhong Shuhuang

Running time
110 minutes

Tang Xiaodan's film was highly popular at the time of its release and was remade in color during the Cultural Revolution. There is even talk of another version being made in 2010. Tang was a veteran of the Chinese movie scene, active since the 1930s – he directed the first "talkie" in Cantonese – and his mastery of the camera is evident. The moonlit scenes in the run up to the fateful swim are shot to perfection, and the battle sequences are effective at building tension. If you're looking for a typical example of what Jiang Wen tried to emulate with his retro war film *Devils on the Doorstep*, this is surely it.

Hong Ying Tao

Red Cherry
1995

As soon as the Chinese film market opened its doors to foreign films, it knew it would have to adapt to compete with the big-budget offerings from Hollywood and Hong Kong. In the 1990s, it began looking abroad for more money, and co-productions with foreign companies and private Chinese firms began. At the same time, ties with Russia and China also began to thaw after their unceremonious political split in the 1960s, allowing for a joint production between the two nations. One such partnership, *Red Cherry*, was on a grand scale, with a budget of 26 million RMB. The gamble paid off for director Ye Daying and the film became the highest grossing in China's history up to that point, beating all foreign competition. It was also nominated for an Oscar, perhaps for its original take on a little-documented episode in the Second World War.

Red Cherry is based on a true story of two Chinese children, Chuchu and Luo Xiaoman, sent to a Russian orphanage for persecuted revolutionaries in 1940. The headmaster at first insists there is no room for them and snot-nosed students push their faces against the windows to see their exotic new classmates. The pair eventually settles in, makes friends and learns Russian. Chuchu takes part in a Russian oral exam and the teacher asks her to speak about her life in China. She first outlines a gentle, happy life, but then tearfully reveals she was forced to watch the Nationalists murder her father.

The encroachment of Germany into Russia forces the orphans to evacuate, but a number of girls are captured by Nazi officers and taken to an abandoned castle. The

Director
Ye Daying

Screenwriter
Jiang Qitao

Cast
Guo Keyu
Xu Xiaoli

Running time
111 minutes

fundamentally evil officers execute the girls' teacher in front of them. One crippled officer imprisons Chuchu, regularly torturing her. His reason? So that she will let him tattoo a German eagle on her back. Reluctantly she agrees, but becomes partially insane over the long, painful process. Luo Xiaoman, meanwhile, remains trapped in a war-torn Moscow. After befriending a girl who talks to her dead mother in bed, Luo assists the resistance. One day, he sees a group of Germans entering a construction site. Antagonizing them by hurling stones at the officers, Luo and his Russian friend lead them deep into the building. Luo sets fire to gas barrels and is killed in the explosion. The war ends and the Russian doctors are unable to remove Chuchu's tattoo. Distraught, she moves back to China to live out the rest of her life.

Despite being filmed mainly in Russian, *Red Cherry* (released with English and Chinese subtitles) was a huge success. Through this film, and other co-productions that followed, Chinese moviegoers were able to learn about other cultures through on-screen portrayals of shared experiences that transcended regional differences.

Chibi

Red Cliff
2008

Director
John Woo

Screenwriters
John Woo
Chen Han
Sheng Heyu

Cinematographers
Lü Yue
Zhang Li

Cast
Tony Leung
  Chiu-Wai
Takeshi Kaneshiro
Zhang Feng Yi
Chang Chen
Zhao Wei
Hu Jun

Running time
280 minutes

At the start of John Woo's career, with movies such as *The Killer* and *Hard Boiled*, he almost single-handedly defined the gritty Hong Kong action flick. Soon Hollywood beckoned, but, despite favorable reviews and returns for films like *Face/Off*, he never quite found his rhythm in the US. As the tides of economic power begin to shift towards the east, he followed the dollars back east and cast his lot in the Chinese Mainland with *Red Cliff*. It is no ordinary John Woo film. Gone are the choreographed, slo-mo gun battles and ruthless Triads, replaced by a meaty period piece of enormous scope (in China it was released in two parts, one in the West) that broke a host of box-office records.

The film is based on one of the most famous battles in Chinese history, the Battle of Red Cliffs, which took place prior to the start of the Three Kingdoms Period and brought a decisive end to the Han dynasty. Unlike other directors who tackle ancient China, Woo aimed at historical accuracy, basing the story on the *Chronicle of the Three Kingdoms* (a third-century account) rather than the popular, embellished version in the classic novel *Romance of the Three Kingdoms*.

Chancellor Cao Cao (*Farewell My Concubine's* Zhang Fengyi) is eager to eliminate warlords San Quan (Chang Chun) and Liu Bei (You Yong), who are plaguing the Eastern Han Dynasty (208 AD). Cao Cao's troops, under the guidance of their overzealous leader, are ruthless, killing civilians as they try to escape the carnage. San Quan and Liu Bei hastily form an alliance to try to hold off the advancing army, which is heading by horseback and boat to Red Cliff – a crucial

"Truth and illusion are often disguised as each other. "

strategic position at the banks of the Yangtze River. The film's first part ends with an amazing bird's eye view (literally) of the immense naval forces assembled, reminiscent of Peter Jackson's depiction of Middle Earth in *Lord of the Rings*. The second film concerns itself with the battle itself, filled with deceit and tactical planning as both armies ready themselves for the epic clash. And it is indeed epic. The final half-hour is a spectacular affair, with Woo opting for a slightly more realistic and bloody depiction of the battle than the usual flying kung fu choreography of most Mainland action films.

The assembled cast – featuring a number of A-list Hong Kong talents – provide the desired gravitas to a film that smashed through the box office in China and abroad. For Woo, whose name is synonymous with Hong Kong action, it's ironic that his greatest international success may in the end come from his films on the Mainland.

Hongse Niangzijun

The Red Detachment of Women
1965

Adapted from the novel of the same name by Liang Xin, *The Red Detachment of Women* is another movie by director Xie Jin that features strong female characters. Although the film was a success, it was the ballet – adapted under the personal direction of Zhou Enlai – that received the most attention when it was performed in front of Richard Nixon during his historic trip to China in 1972. The film, as Chairman Mao would have put it, is proof that women "hold up half of the sky" and that their input was just as necessary as their male counterparts if true revolution was to be achieved. Nowadays, the words *hongse niangzijun* have come mean a tough, domineering older woman.

The film takes place on Hainan Island, off the coast of Guangxi Province, where Wu Qionghua is kept as a slave by Nan Baitian – played by Chen Qiang with his usual fervor – a ruthless landlord who killed her father. Relentless, Wu had tried to escape on many occasions only to be captured and tortured. A foil to the gaunt, pale landlord, Hong Changqing is a well-groomed Communist agent disguised as an Overseas-Chinese arms dealer. Hong negotiates for the release of Wu and integrates her into a female detachment of the army. Like any good heroine in a genre movie, she has only one thing on her mind: revenge. Her outlandish attempts to kill Nan, who has a large army at his disposal, bring her fellow soldiers and the revolutionary cause into danger. With time and with instruction in the tenants of communism, she channels her rage into something constructive for the revolution. When Hong is exposed as being as a Communist

Director
Xie Jin

Screenwriter
Liang Xin

Cast
Zhu Xijuan
Wang Xingang
Chen Qiang

Running time
110 minutes

"You can cut off my head, but you can't kill my Communist beliefs."

agent, he is imprisoned in the same jail that once held Wu. Lurking outside the landlord's property, Wu leads a successful assault and captures it for the good of the party. Although Hong is killed, Wu marches the army into battle without him. The Hainan of the movie serves as a microcosm for China, and much is left to be done if the Communists are going to win the fight.

The filmed version of the ballet – one of the Eight Model Ballets permitted during the Cultural Revolution – remains more popular, but this version is richer in detail and emotional depth, and should be remembered as one of the pivotal movies in the lead up to the Cultural Revolution. Xie's visual style is arresting and, for generations of Chinese, his socialist realism would come to typify what movie making meant.

CHEN QIANG

Chen played the villain so often that it started to affect his personal life. He portrayed the evil landlord in The White-Haired Girl *(both the play and film) and also the dastardly general in* The Red Detachment of Women. *The public often couldn't distinguish between the on and off-screen personalities. People used to throw fruit at him as he walked down the street and once a soldier even pointed a gun at him.*

151

Hongxia

Red Heroine
1928

Red Heroine is a noble work of art, but by proxy. In the 1920s and '30s, much like today, the Chinese film market was flooded with epic kung fu tales. The prince among these was *The Burning of the Red Lotus Temple*, a film so grand it is sometimes credited as being the longest film ever made (clocking in at 27 hours long, it was shown in several parts between 1928 and 1931). Its director, Zhang Shichuan (*Cheng the Fruit Seller*), was a trailblazer in Chinese cinema, but his finest work remains the subject of conjecture, as not a single shred of *The Burning of the Red Lotus Temple* exists today.

Red Heroine has the dubious honor of being a copycat of *Red Lotus* that has outlasted the original, but only one of its 13 original parts remains. So why include it? Of the 200-odd kung fu genre films made in China between 1927 and 1931, it's the only one that exists in entirety. It can therefore give hints about a vast body of dramatic, exciting Chinese cinema, which we would otherwise know virtually nothing about.

The film stars Wen Yumin (who also directs) as the White Monkey, a mysterious Taoist hermit and the protector of female lead Yun Mei. Yun Mei is kidnapped by a gang of local bandits but is rescued by the White Monkey. Three years pass and under the tutelage of the White Monkey, Yun Mei has been transformed into the eponymous fighting Red Heroine, with the ability to fly and a strong sense of justice. She attacks the band of renegades' lair – a cross between the bar in the Mos Eisley scene in *Star Wars* and an old China

Director
Wen Yimin

Cast
Fan Xuepeng
Shu Gohui
Wang Juqing
Wen Yimin
Sao Guanyu

Running time
94 minutes

strip joint (yes, even with partial nudity!) – dispatching the villains with consummate ease using the methods that later became the stock and trade of martial art films.

What's interesting about *Red Heroine*, and we assume most martial art films of this period, is the moralistic sense of justice and honor visible throughout (the martial arts genre is known in Chinese as *wuxia* or "honorable, chivalrous"). It also contains another archetype that has continued to saturate the genre, being visible in contemporary works like *Kill Bill*, the pious and restrained master teaching the younger apprentice his art and code. *Red Heroine* may not be the film we want it to be, but it's still rich and lively, and warrants attention as an important precursor to the worldwide kung fu phenomenon.

153

Red Sorghum
1987

Hong Gaoliang

Zhang Yimou had already made a significant contribution to Chinese cinema before directing his first feature film. His work as a cinematographer on the films of other Fifth Generation luminaries had garnered much attention. But when it came time for him to direct his own feature, it was in an actress and not a camera where he found his creative inspiration. Gong Li's early career is synonymous with Zhang's work, each taking the other to new heights – it's as if they were destined to be together. Their much-publicized off-screen romance no doubt played a role, but Gong Li's strength, personal courage and flawless execution in films such as *To Live* and *Red Sorghum* marked the beginning of the most fruitful relationship in modern Chinese cinema.

The name says it all. Zhang Yimou's obsession with color is well known, and in this film the red of the sorghum comes to represent love, life and – most vividly for a Chinese movie – sexuality. Narrated by the protagonist's grandson, the film opens as Jiu'er (Gong Li) is being carried apprehensively towards her wedding, the vivid reds of the procession contrasting strongly with the bleak surroundings. She admires the bare-chested men with surreptitious glances, far cries from the decrepit old leper to whom she has been sold into marriage. On the journey, a masked robber stops the procession. The leader of the procession rescues Jiu'er and takes the other men on a rampage that claims the life of the assailant.

On another journey sometime later, Jiu'er is kidnapped by a masked man in the sorghum field. It transpires that the

Director
Zhang Yimou

Screenwriter
Mo Yan (novel)

Cast
Gong Li
Jiang Wen
Ten Rujun
Jia Liu

Running time
91 minutes

masked man is none other than the man who previously saved her life. He tramples a clearing in the field and rapes Jiu'er. From the incident comes a child (the narrator's father), and the sedan-carrier-turned-rapist kills Jiu'er's husband and takes her as his wife. Together, they take over the running of a liquor distillery. This strange union is complicated with the arrival of the Japanese, who turn the sorghum field into a place of desolation, forcing the locals to build a road through it. After the Japanese kill a Communist rebel, Jiu'er inspires the men to rebel against them. In a highly stylized slow-motion sequence, the villagers battle against the Japanese, but are ultimately unsuccessful. Jiu'er and many others are killed, their blood mingling with the soil and the sorghum.

Gong Li's sexuality in the film is startling; the antithesis of the fawning, meek femininity that characterized females in earlier Chinese films. Gu Changwei's photography is rich in meaning: life, death, love and lust all symbolized by the blood red sorghum field. Zhang began his directing career to critical acclaim and would go on, with Gong Li as his greatest muse, to envision some of the finest moments in Chinese cinematic history.

Rickshaw Boy
1982

Luotuo Xiangzi

Director
Ling Zifeng

Screenwriters
Ling Zifeng
Lao She (novel)

Cast
Zhang Fengyi
Yin Xin
Yan Bide
Siqin Gaowa
Li Xiang

Running time
117 minutes

Poor Xiangzi. The hero of *Rickshaw Boy* yearns for a simple life. Hard work, dedication and honest behavior should surely be the path to a modest existence. Alas, this is most definitely not the case in this heart-wrenching adaptation of a Chinese classic.

From the outset, Xiangzi just wants to earn an honest living. As a peasant growing up in the 1920s, he comes to Beijing to seek work and finds a job as a rickshaw driver. After three years of toil, he buys his own cart. But it is a time of political instability, and Xiangzi is caught in the middle. He is conscripted into a local warlord's army, using his rickshaw to transport ammunition. The army is thoroughly defeated and his prized rickshaw is lost. A peculiarity of fate leads Xiangzi to three roaming camels (hence the source novel's original English-language title: *Camel Xiangzi*), which he sells for 35 *kuai*. He cleans himself up, buying new clothes and cutting his hair, but he still returns to rickshaw pulling.

The rickshaw company boss and his unmarried daughter, Huniu, run the operation with an iron fist. It's not long, however, before Huniu falls in love with the humble Xiangzi. Although her feelings aren't mutual, Xiangzi is seduced into sleeping with her and, out of shame, he leaves to work for another company. His new employer is a leftist intellectual, who becomes entangled with the authorities, and the luckless Xiangzi loses his life savings in the ensuing commotion. Xiangzi reluctantly returns to live with Huniu after she tricks him into believing that she is pregnant. They marry, but her father does not approve of the union

156

and they are forced to move across the city. They eventually conceive a child, but Huniu miscarries and dies. In the final and perhaps bleakest section of the film, Xiangzi, with newly accumulated savings, falls in love with a young girl who was forced into prostitution by her father. When he arrives at the brothel to purchase her freedom, he discovers that she has already killed herself.

Xiangzi's resilience endears him to the audience, but his situation is hopeless. As Lao She's original novel preaches, 1920s Chinese society is the real villain. The score, like the protagonist, plods along with a stoic magnificence, perfectly highlighting the film's melancholic tone. The cinematography relies on silhouettes and shadows, crafting a film that is as easy on the eye as it is hard on the heart. It still remains one of the finest examples of the socialist realist style that was already drifting out of popularity by the early 1980s.

Nongnu

Serfs
1963

Although China's ethnic groups sporadically appeared in films like *Romance in Yao Mountains* (1933) and *Storm on the Border* (1940), it wasn't until the Communist Revolution that a distinct minority cinematic genre began to appear. The main purpose of films like *Serfs* was to show that class struggle was not something that only affected Han Chinese, and that the traditions and beliefs of China's 55 ethnic minorities should be integrated into the greater Han population.

Serfs is a none-too-subtle exploration of this theme. Made 12 years after the "liberation" of Tibet, the film highlights the alarming plight that some Tibetans faced in the pre-Communist era. Whereas other Chinese films sought to glamorize minority groups by depicting them happily singing and dancing, *Serfs* shows a marginalized and downtrodden Tibetan people. The jarring contrast between the hardworking peasants and the cleanly dressed elite is stark, and through the mistreatment of the latter by the former, we are left with no doubt that – for the Tibetans at least – anyone who would split Tibet from China is an enemy.

The film opens as two serfs are killed by their master shortly after our hero, Jampa, was born. Raised by his grandmother, Jampa is forced to act as a human horse for his master's son. This role, along with general barbaric mistreatment, forces Jampa to become more and more introverted, confiding only in his pal Gezong and his sister Lamka. He stops speaking and is believed to be mute. Gezong contacts People's Liberation Army soldiers (hurrah!), who help him recover from the cruel treatment. Energized with the

Director
Li Jun

Screenwriter
Huang Zongjiang

Cast
Wang Dui
Huang Zongjiang
Jangje, Brima
Tsering, Doje
Yange Padma

Running time
85 minutes

hope of liberation, Jampa, Gezong and Lamka join the army. Their efforts are initially successful, but Jampa is captured and given to the living Buddha, Thubtan, who pretends to support the Chinese but is actually a splittist working with Jampa's former master, Namchal. Eventually the serfs rise up against their feudal overlords. Namchal flees and takes Jampa with him to once again serve as a human horse. Jampa escapes to warn the PLA of Namchal and Thubtan's plans. Scared of exposure, Thubtan starts a fire that nearly kills Jampa, but Jampa survives and discovers a weapons cache in Thubtan's temple. Jampa magically regains his speech and, in the closing shot, he mouths the words "Mao Zedong" while looking at the Great Helmsman's image.

The film takes full advantage of Tibet's wondrous landscape, complimented by an inventive mix of Tibetan and Western-Chinese music. As you'd expect from Li Jun – who would go on to make the red-hot *Sparkling Red Star* – there is no moral gray area. The film depicts Tibetans as helpless and backwards. Those looking to reaffirm their political views will take something from this film, but ideologically this movie does little more than take a big anti-splittist stick and beat you over the head with it.

Xizao

Shower
1999

Director
Zhang Yang

Screenwriters
Liu Fendou
Cai Xiangjun
Diao Yinan
Huo Xin
Yang Zhang

Cast
Zhu Xu
Pu Cunxin
Jiang Wu
He Zeng
Zhang Jinhao
Lao Lin
Lao Wu

Running time
111 minutes

A lot of films in this anthology move at a frantic pace, as if the severity of the images was required to justify the films' content. Refreshingly, *Shower* is a much gentler film, moving at a slow and sedate tempo. The film's rhythm is entirely intentional, as Zhang Yang aims to portray the often-overlooked customs in a Beijing bathhouse – a place where old-timers come to relax and enjoy a scrub, massage, shave and other personal pamperings.

The opening scene provides contrast for the rest of the film. Liu Daming is a slick urbanite in a flashy suit in the moneyed city of Shenzhen. He enters a mechanized booth called "The Amazing Automatic Shower", inserts a few coins and receives an express version of the full bathhouse treatment. It's comedic but at its heart reflects a serious point: in China's rush to develop, people have stopped taking the time to fully appreciate the cherished aspects of their culture. Daming's father, whom he rarely visits, Da Liu, runs a traditional bathhouse in Beijing. Daming decides to return home when he receives a cryptic postcard from his mentally challenged brother, Erming, wrongly implying that his father has died. Daming's lifestyle is out of step with the bathhouse patrons, who seek solace in a slow-paced life and sanctuary from the outside world. Erming may be a little slow but he is still attentive and sensitive to the needs of the patrons, and Da Liu depends upon him to keep the place running smoothly. One day, when Erming is separated from his brother and becomes lost in town, Da Liu says he has "already lost one son" and can't afford to lose another.

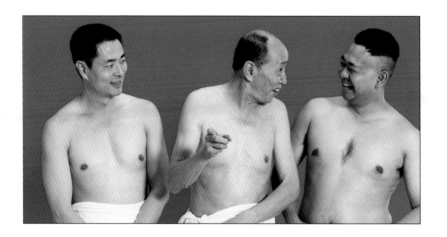

Luckily, Erming finds his way home the next morning and the relieved Daming delays his return. At first begrudging them, Daming learns the daily chores of the bathhouse and eventually takes pleasure in them. He decides to put off his return to Shenzhen once more.

It's soon revealed that the old bathhouse is to be demolished to make way for a new shopping mall. The evening after city employees come around to survey the building (the Chinese censors had this scene deleted from the film's release in China), Da Liu dies peacefully in his sleep while bathing. Erming refuses to accept that the bathhouse and the buildings surrounding it must make way for the construction company. Daming considers taking Erming back to live with him in Shenzhen, but, fearing his wife's reaction, decides instead to have him committed to a mental hospital. When the nurses come to take him away, Erming struggles and demands to be taken back to the bathhouse. Even as the demolition crew arrives, Erming attempts to fend them off, but in this story there are no fairytale endings and Erming, Daming and the bathhouse regulars must accept the fate of their beloved institution, leveled in the name of progress.

Sanqiang Pai'an Jingqi

A Simple Noodle Story
1999

How on earth did this happen? Zhang Yimou rebounds from the dire *Curse of the Golden Flower* with a remake of the Coen Brother's *Blood Simple*? Zhang had often stated his admiration for their movies in interviews, but few thought he would do a remake their dark and brooding 1984 cinematic debut. Zhang transposed the gritty Texan bar of *Blood Simple* into a noodle restaurant in northwest China. Rather than replicate the noirish feel of the original, Zhang choose a period setting and divided the film (tonally) into two separate parts: comedy and drama. Stylistically, Zhang remains infatuated with color schemes, but other than that, *A Simple Noodle Story* is his most significant stylistic departure since *The Story of Qiu Jin*.

Wang Mazi (Ni Dahong) is the proprietor of the noodle shop that he runs with his wife (Yan Ni) and the effeminate Li Si (Xiao Shenyang). A pair of bumbling servants, Zhao Liu (Cheng Ye) and Chen Qi (Mao Mao), provides most of the film's comedic energy in the opening half. When Wang's wife purchases a gun from some traveling Persian salesmen, the staff becomes suspicious of her intentions. The Persians test fire a cannon, immediately bringing a corrupt police officer, Zhang (Sun Hunglei), into the dusty town. Zhang discovers Wang's wife and Li are having an affair and breaks the news to Wang. Wanting revenge, Wang hires Zhang to kill the lovers, but we soon learn he has his own agenda. Sticking faithfully to nearly every twist, turn and betrayal in the original, the film also provides comedic flourishes with regional humor, slapstick and quickly spoken regional dialect.

Director
Zhang Yimou

Screenwriters
Shi Jianquan
Shang Jing

Cast
Sun Honglei
Ni Dahong
Xiao Shenyang
Yan Ni

Running time
111 minutes

With stunning views of the northwest, *A Simple Noodle Story* is a beautiful film, but the broad performances from the likes of Xiao Shenyang – who had made a name for himself in an infamous sketch that appeared on TV where he played a highly camp character who was allegedly homosexual – might be a little too much for Western audiences. But, judging by the success of films like *A Simple Noodle Story* and *Crazy Stone*, over-the-top is just the way the Chinese like it.

Yeban Gesheng

Song at Midnight
1937

Often described as China's first horror movie, *Song at Midnight* is an atmospheric interpretation of Gaston Leroux's novel *The Phantom of the Opera*. Horror has traditionally been an undersubscribed genre in China, with more emphasis placed on melodramatic tragedy than spook stories. For a first crack, *Song at Midnight* is rather well developed. Lit predominantly by candlelight, there's an eerie quality about the characters as they move in and out of shots. Their voices, too, have an otherworldly quality as they mutter and cackle through the scenes; the impressive baritone of the phantom (Jin Shan) is particularly haunting. This being a Chinese movie, there is also a hint of social criticism in the mix.

The film is set in a chilling old theater where a group of actors set up shop for a series of performances. During rehearsals, the leading man, Sun, receives a helping hand from a ghostly figure. Sun discovers that the ghost is in fact Song, a well-known revolutionary figure who disguised himself as an actor to escape capture. A decade earlier, Song was in love with the beautiful Miss Li. Unluckily for him, the town rogue – who also had a soft spot for Miss Li – poured acid on his face. Not wanting to be seen in public, Song faked his own death, but the news was too much for Miss Li, who was driven to insanity by grief. Song now spends night after night singing to her, and decides that if he can get Sun to visit Miss Li, it may aid in her recovery. But just as things are starting to go well, the thug who deformed Song returns for the film's dramatic coda.

Director
Ma Xu Weibang

Screenwriter
Ma Xu Weibang

Cast
Jin Shan
Gu Menghe
Zhou Wenzhu
Hu Ping

Running time
113 minutes

"Only by singing at midnight, can I banish your loneliness."

Song at Midnight uses many horror staples to create its spine-tingling scenes: shadows, abandoned buildings, thin hands emerging through cobwebs. The film was hugely successful at the box office and Ma Xu Weibang went on to direct a number of other horror films such as *Walking Corpse in an Old House* and *The Lonely Soul*. In 1941, a sequel to the *Song at Midnight* was made, but didn't enjoy the same success. Other directors, especially in Hong Kong, took cues from the film and it has been remade again and again (most recently in the 1990s), proving that although it may have only been the first of a small number of Chinese horror films, it is evidently the best. The score of *Song at Midnight* was also popular and influential. Composer Nie Er went on to produce the music for the film *Children of the Storm*, the main theme of which became the national anthem of the People's Republic of China.

THE HORROR
Horror has never been a hugely popular genre in China and it looks like the thin canon of horror films might not develop for a while. In 2006, China's censorship body (the State Administration of Radio, Film and Television, or SARFT) imposed a ban on all films containing "unhealthy" or "excessive" scenes of horror.

165

Yu Guang Qu

Song of the Fishermen
1937

Song of the Fishermen was China's most internationally well known film in the 1930s. It was the first Chinese film to win an award at an international film festival ("Honorable Mention" at the 1935 Moscow Film Festival) and the highest grossing film in Chinese history for many years. Despite the Nationalist government's attempt to censor it, and an unusually hot summer in Shanghai that kept many cinemagoers away, the film ran for 84 days after its release on June 14, 1934.

Writer/director Cai Chusheng's portrayal of the lives of Chinese fishermen is told with an eerie feeling of disquiet. Like other leftist films of the '30s, *Song of the Fishermen* highlights the miserable and often tragic lives of China's working class, and the need for them to unify and fight for their survival.

After briefly introducing fisherman Xu and his family, the film repeatedly shows the ominous shadows cast by the wet nurse as she tends to newborn twins Monkey (male) and Kitten (female). When Xu, the breadwinner, dies, his wife is forced to become a wet nurse for He Ziying, the son of wealthy local fisherman. The twins and Ziying grow up together, unaware of the financial disparity that separates them. When the twins are of age they follow in their father's footsteps and begin fishing, while Ziying goes abroad to study new techniques for catching fish. Unwittingly, the twins' outdated methods are forced to compete with Ziying's modernized approach. Seeking work, the twins move to Shanghai – much in the same way as Sister Ye in *Little Toys* – but they end up foraging for scrap and singing songs on

Director
Cai Chusheng

Screenwriter
Cai Chusheng

Cast
Wang Renmei
Yuan Congmei
Han Lan'gen,
Tang Tianxiu

Running time
57 minutes

166

street corners for money. By chance, Ziying discovers Kitten on the street and gives her a 100 yuan note, but the money is more trouble than it's worth. Kitten is picked up by the police, suspicious as to why she has such a large amount of money. The twins manage to clear their names, only to learn that their mother – upset at the news of their arrest – accidentally started a fire, killing both herself and their uncle. Wealth cannot insulate Ziying from tragedy, either, and he soon learns that an untrustworthy mistress has bankrupted his father. Ziying's father takes his own life and leaves Ziying as destitute as his childhood friends. The trio bands together, returns home and restarts their fishing business, offering a sliver of a chance at redemption.

The impressionistic cinematography in *Song of the Fishermen* helps it achieve more artistic success than other films made of its time, but its real strength lies in its populist message. Its perspective on the plight of rural Chinese communities was hardly original, but the sheer volume of Chinese moviegoers who flocked to watch it shows that its themes strongly resonated with ordinary Chinese people.

Caoyuan Ernü

Sons and Daughters of the Grassland
1974

Sons and Daughters of the Grassland is quite possibly the campiest Chinese film ever made. It also has the dubious honor of being one of only a handful of films released during the Cultural Revolution (1966-76). The Gang of Four (the leaders of the movement) and Mao Zedong were locked in a power struggle for China and, as a result, many artists and intellectuals – including many in the film industry – were denunciated and/or sent into exile. But the need for entertainment was always there and, fearing stories that could be construed as critical of the government, Mao's wife, former film starlet Jiang Qing, supervised the recording of several "model operas" and ballets at Beijing Film Studios.

The story behind *Sons and Daughters of the Grassland* is simple enough: a Mongolian boy and girl defend a flock of sheep from the harsh elements. Thrown in is a stock capitalist villain who tries to sabotage the efforts of the girls, but they prevail, sacrificing themselves for the good of the collective. The story comes from a real-life tale of two sisters from Inner Mongolia who helped their father by grazing sheep on the grasslands. Suddenly, a snowstorm scared the sheep away. Realizing the importance of the sheep to the community, the sisters (aged 9 and 11, respectively), followed them for more than 30 hours. The girls were rescued but they both lost toes and one lost a leg due to frostbite. Another influence was a cartoon based on the story, *Heroic Little Sisters of the Grassland* (1964), but to keep with operatic conventions, a male-female relationship was inserted at its core.

Director
Fu Jie

Screenwriters
China Dancing
 Group

Cast
Zhang Chunzeng
Cai Guobo
Huang Minxuan
Song Chen
Wu Kunsen

Running time
68 minutes

168

"The stars in the sky are countless, more than the sheep in our community. Our dearest Chairman, you bring us a bright future."

Although set in Inner Mongolia's verdant grasslands (complete with electricity pylons), all action was filmed on a sound stage. Intercut with startling crash zooms and overly sincere performances, *Sons and Daughters* almost feels like a parody. The climax, which owes much to Peking opera, will probably leave you thinking it's a spoof, but it isn't.

The ballet was hugely popular when released, blending "ethnic" dancing with strong nationalist imagery. The dashing People's Liberation Army soldiers, who intermittently turn up to save the day, are at least 6 inches taller than everyone else in the film. Slightly less impressive is the flock of sheep, represented by a single glassy-eyed puppet that meekly dances across the scenery. But this absurdity only enhances the enjoyment of this otherworldly film – where ballerinas smile as they leap through the countryside, in stark contrast to the tough reality facing the Chinese off-screen.

MODEL OPERAS
The "Eight Model Operas" were politically themed operas and ballets performed during the Cultural Revolution. Despite the name, there were actually more like 15, the most popular being The Red Detachment of Women, *a Beijing opera made famous when it was performed in front of Richard Nixon during his visit to China in February 1972.*

Shanshan de Hongxing

Sparkling Red Star
1974

In so many ways, Dongzi, the pre-teen lead in *Sparkling Red Star*, is the archetypal children's movie hero: a Huckleberry Finn-esque character with a penchant for adventure and mischief. What sets him (and the film) apart from the finest Disney schmaltz is the way he sets an evil community-tormenting landlord on fire and kills him with an axe. The young Mao-quoting lad isn't actually atypical of the Cultural Revolution era, when China was overrun with sometimes violent radical youths. The tone of the film is by turns shocking, exciting and amusing, but never when it intends to be.

Set in the 1930s – when China was struggling against the Japanese – *Sparkling Red Star* is utterly relentless in its political message. Whereas films in previous decades spread the socialist message through symbolism and metaphor, *Sparkling Red Star* is straightforward – the dialogue is almost entirely composed of Party doctrine, bashing you over the head with jingoism and slogans to an extent that it becomes tiring.

Dongzi is obsessed with the Red Army and the Communist Party, even more so when his father goes away to fight with them. As his father leaves, he gives Dongzi the eponymous Red Star, promising that when he returns he will be able to join the revolutionary struggle. Dongzi is young but sharp as a whip, outwitting the Japanese forces and the local landlord (a caricature class enemy). His mother is killed by the evil landlord and his soldiers, but her martyrdom only fuels his love for Chairman Mao and the Communists.

Directors
Li Jun
Li Ang

Screenwriters
Lu Zhugao
Wang Yuanchien
Li Xintian (novel)

Starring
Zhu Xinyun
Gao Baocheng
Liu Jiang
Li Xuehong

Running time
100 minutes

"Hey, let's play the game: 'Beat up the Landlord'."

He kills the landlord and, when his father returns, Dongzi is deemed ready to join the front line.

The film creates a rich visual tapestry with genuinely moving cinematography. The color red saturates every scene, and directors Li Jun and Li Ang fill every shot with impassioned faces. The film is pure propaganda, best viewed from today's cultural and political distance, but unmatched as an historical document. The closing shot sums it up perfectly: the men praise Chairman Mao after their victory and the camera pans to the setting sun. The image of Chairman Mao, "the red sun in our hearts", is unmistakable, often used through Chinese Communist cinema.

Xiaocheng zhi Chun

Spring in a Small Town
1948

Spring in a Small Town is widely considered the greatest Chinese-language film ever made; the Chinese *Citizen Kane*, if you will. But its "classic" status has only really been achieved since the 1980s, because at the time of its release the Communist government dismissed the film for its "decadence", "backwardness" and the "narcotic effect" it had on audiences during a time of war. Compared to other films of the time, it's easy to see what would have riled the Communist government. Film, for them, was the tool of communicating the party's ideals and philosophies, and the majority of the cinematic output during the 1940s and '50s was explicitly political. *Spring in a Small Town* is much more concerned with the psychology of its characters, and politics serve merely as a backdrop to the drama as it unfolds.

Set in a small, unidentified town in south China, the protagonists live in a rundown house surrounded by the ruined city wall, which – like the main characters – suffered greatly during the war. Zhou Yuwen (Wei Wei), the film's narrator, has been married to Dai Liyan (Shi Yu) for eight loveless years, during which time he has been gravely ill. They live with Liyan's excitable younger sister, Dai Xiu (Zhang Hongmei), and the loyal house-servant Lao Huang (Cui Chaoming). Nothing changes in their existence; Liyan wallows in convalescence and Yuwen virtuously takes care of him. Then, with the arrival of springtime, a ghost from the past returns to their lives: Li Wei (Zhang Zhichen), a childhood friend of Liyan and Yuwen's former lover. Now a doctor, Li Wei is taken in by the family, stirring up strong yet previously

Director
Fei Mu

Screenwriter
Li Tianji

Starring
Wei Wei
Shi Yu
Li Wei
Cui Chaoming
Zhang Hongmei

Running time
85 minutes

dormant feelings in Yuwen. The three players in the love triangle are all bound by a strict moral code, yet at times the sexual desire Zhou Yuwen feels for her lost beau is palpable – she kneads the buttons on her clothing frantically when they are alone together, but they never allow themselves to give into their desires. When Liyan realizes what is going on, he attempts to kill himself. He is unsuccessful, but makes Li Wei and Yuwen reconsider their potential affair. Just as quickly as he entered their life, Li Wei is gone and family life, however unhappy, continues as before.

The film turned out to be director Fei Mu's swan song; he died a few years later without making another film. Although it spent years in the wilderness, the affection that is felt towards this film is great, and Fei has in the time since its release become hailed as one of the greatest directors of the pre-Communist era. The film's detached and cool visual style creates feelings of dread and, at times, menace. It is also revolutionary in its representation of women in Chinese society. Wei Wei's character symbolizes the Confucian ideal of a doting and noble wife, but her pronounced sexuality also hints at a more modern idea of femininity. The film smolders and bubbles with rich symbolism and depth, and has rightly earned the accolades that have been heaped upon it.

Yi Jiang Chunshui Xiang Dong

A Spring River Flows East
1947

A film that achieves success in its own time is one thing, but to be considered a great work 60 years later is something else entirely. *A Spring River Flows East* has done both: the film was wildly successful in 1947, selling out most cinemas during its three-month Shanghai run in Shanghai and ranking high on most critics' lists of the best Chinese movies of the last century. The melodrama which it came to symbolize became intensely popular in Taiwan and Hong Kong, where the genre dominated until the 1970s. The story contrasts the corruption of a man with the misfortunes of his family, and speaks out against the poor conditions suffered by the general populace under the Kuomintang government. Divided into two parts – *Eight War-torn Years* and *The Dawn* – the film was the zenith of the working partnership of directors Cai Chusheng and Zheng Junli.

The first half is set in pre-war Shanghai and deals with the early life and marriage of Sufen (Bai Yang) and Zhang Zhongliang (Tao Jin). The couple works in a textile factory, where Zhongliang raises funds for an army fighting against the Japanese in northeast China. They marry and have a child, but when the Japanese reach Shanghai, Zhongliang retreats to Chongqing and joins the resistance. He leaves his wife, son and mother behind in Shanghai, where they are persecuted at the hands of the Japanese. In Chongqing, he meets up with an old female acquaintance, Wang Lizhen. He resists at first, but it's not long before he becomes accustomed to the luxurious bourgeois lifestyle. The first part ends as Sufen, now working in a refugee camp, is drenched by a heavy storm.

Directors
Cai Chusheng
Zheng Junli

Screenwriters
Cai Chusheng
Zheng Junli

Cast
Bai Yang
Shu Xiuwen
Wu Yin
Shangguan Yunzhu
Tao Jin

Running time
192 minutes

The second part opens with Zhongliang, now a successful entrepreneur, marrying Lizhen. Sufen remains in the refugee camp until the Japanese dismantle it and force her and her son, now a little boy, to look for work. She takes a job as a maid in a wealthy family's home, which happens to be where Zhongliang and Lizhen live. During a cocktail party held to celebrate National Day, Sufen spies Zhongliang dancing with Lizhen and drops her tray in horror. The fallout leaves everyone shaken and, on learning that she must divorce her husband, Sufen drowns herself at the docks.

The film strongly advocates the family unit as a metaphor for how the Chinese people should stick together. Zhongliang's mother in the film is a typical Chinese matriarch, with strong convictions and plenty of good advice. On the other hand is the vampish Lizhen, whose Western clothing and pronounced sexuality mark her out as a wrong'un, a trollop any sensible man should surely leave well alone. The role of Sufen, along with her work in *Crossroads*, helped propel Bai Yang to stardom. Tragically, as with many leading artists of the era, politics would prevent her from ever reaching the same heights as she did in the '30s and '40s.

Chuncan

Spring Silkworms
1933

The credits for *Spring Silkworms* read like a *Who's Who* of 1930s Chinese leftist intellectuals. Mao Dun, upon whose short story the film is based, is known as one of the finest writers in the realist genre and would go on to become Minister of Culture of China from 1949 to 1965. Mao penned *Spring Silkworms* in 1932 and Xia Yan, a member of an underground Communist organization, adapted the work for the screen. From there it was given to Cheng Bugao, one of China's most prolific directors of all time, to realize Mao Dun's vision. Cheng used his own humanist approach to explore the everyday trials and tribulations of the rural population, creating a classic of Chinese silent cinema.

Spring Silkworms opens in a small village in rural Zhejiang province, where the main industry, cultivating silkworms, comes under direct competition from foreign industrial nations. Tongbao and his family slave and come up with various plans in order to make their crop of silkworms more healthy and productive, but they are superstitious and often hindered by nature. Hehua is a local woman believed to bring bad luck, and Tongbao is adamant that his son should not be playing with her, because of the disastrous consequences it could have for the harvest. Angry at his father's meddling, Tongbao's son throws a handful of his silkworms into the river.

This symbolic act foreshadows a change in the village's fortunes, as a low yield of silkworms leads to debt, and they must find new and innovative ways of producing more and more silkworms. When Tongbao sets off to a neighboring

Director
Cheng Bugao

Screenwriters
Cai Chusheng
Xia Yan

Cast
Xiao Ying
Gong Jianong
Zheng Xiaoqiu
Gao Qianping
Ai Xia

Running time
96 minutes

village, he finds the local shop closed due to heavy fighting between local warlords. The search for alternative ways to sell his products forces Tongbao further afield, but he is met with fierce competition that forces him to sell at much lower rates. Although he and his family struggle to pull themselves out of debt, they remain trapped in an unrelenting cycle. His family's poverty, which he is helpless to prevent, causes Tongbao to become greatly depressed.

Although its style was somewhat different, *Spring Silkworms* contained many of the same themes as Chinese films of the same period: rural endeavor crushed at the hands of external competition and the inherent goodness of hard work. Director Cheng Bugao was originally a film critic who started directing because of his dissatisfaction with the standard of Chinese movies. By adopting a naturalistic "documentary" approach, he pioneered a new style of Chinese filmmaking.

Sanxia Haoren

Still Life
2006

In *Still Life*, Jia Zhangke tells an astonishing story based upon real events surrounding the construction of the Three Gorges Dam. The project was set up to create the world's largest hydroelectric power station, but in its wake, it submerged entire towns and displaced more than 1.5 million people. While construction was going on, Jia brought his cameras to Fengjie, Sichuan, a town upriver from the dam, and produced a low-fi story about a town about to be flooded.

While the town is literally being demolished, Sanming (Jia's cousin Han Sanming), a coal miner from Shanxi, comes looking for his wife – whom he "purchased" 16 years ago – and his daughter. All he has is an address scribbled down on an old cigarette pack, but he soon discovers that the entire area has already been flooded. With no real leads, he takes up work tearing down buildings for 40 RMB a day while he continues to look for his estranged family. Shen Hong (Zhao Tao) is also in town looking for her husband Guo Bing, who has become a successful businessman since she last saw him. During her search, she discovers that he has begun an affair with a wealthy investor. The city is literally collapsing around them, with the character (*chai*, meaning "tear down") painted on everything along with red lines indicating the future water level when the next phase of the dam's construction is complete.

Told at Jia's typically sedate pace, the film's setting is truly remarkable. Only in China is such large-scale upheaval conceivable, let alone possible. The two characters convey a deep emotional distress (despite the obvious flaws

Director
Jia Zhangke

Screenwriters
Jia Zhangke
Guan Na
Sun Jiamin

Cinematographer
Yuk Likwai

Cast
Jiao Tao
Han Sanming
Wang Hongwei

Running time
108 minutes

"Present-day society doesn't suit us because we're too nostalgic."

in their marriages), as they try to salvage something of the relationship in an environment that is also rapidly deteriorating. Jia is a master at portraying the difficulties of communities in flux, as in his debut *Pickpocket*. Ever increasing in confidence, there are a brilliant flourishes of surrealism in the film – a large building structure takes off like a spaceship, three actors in full Peking opera regalia sit at a dinner table playing cards. These images, although incongruous, demonstrate Jia's obsession with the interaction between the old and new worlds. He offers no answers for how these worlds can coexist, but instead highlights the immediate struggles this transition places on working-class Chinese. Jia lets his images do the talking and the wondrous, desolate scenes are beautifully shot by Jia's frequent cinematographic partner, Yuk Likwai.

DONG

At the same time he was producing Still Life, *Jia Zhangke produced another film,* Dong. *It is an hour-long documentary about artist Liu Xiaodong, director of the film* Beijing Bastards *and star of Wang Xiaoshuai's* The Days. *The film explores more directly the Three Gorges Dam project, as Liu Xiaodong paints pictures of the workers being paid to demolish the houses in Fengjie. It is well worth watching and a brilliant companion piece to* Still Life.

179

The Story of Qiu Ju
1992

Qiu Ju Da Guan Si

The consensus was unanimous. Despite having collaborated so successfully in previous films, Zhang Yimou's decision to cast Gong Li as a lowly peasant in his latest film was a big mistake. Friends had confided in him their fears. Liu Heng, who was adapting his own novel for the screenplay, telephoned Zhang to express his doubts, saying he was consumed by writer's block when he thought about writing the part for her. Even Zhang – as he later recalled – was only about 60 percent sure he was making the right decision. Was his personal relationship with Gong beginning to cloud his judgment?

But casting was not the only risk Zhang was willing to take in *The Story of Qiu Ju*. Realizing that his trademark aesthetic with vivid, stylized images would be out of place in a film about a woman's struggle against petty bureaucracy, Zhang dispensed with his usual procedure of storyboarding every scene (he'd learned at the Beijing Film Academy that *all* the greats did this), and instead relied on hidden cameras and untrained actors speaking regional Shaanxi dialect. His intuitions were well founded: Gong Li was awarded best actress at the Venice Film Festival and Zhang, who to this day is highly self-critical, considers it his most complete work as a director.

Qiu Ju (Gong Li) is a visibly pregnant peasant farmer living with her husband in a small village in Shaanxi (which is, incidentally, where Zhang Yimou grew up). One day, Qiu's husband, Qinglai, is engaging in an innocent conversation with the head of the community, Wang Shantang. Qinglai

Director
Zhang Yimou

Screenwriter
Liu Heng

Cast
Gong Li
Liu Peiqi

Running time
100 minutes

180

accidentally implies that Wang is unable to father a male heir and Wang is so offended he savagely beats Qinglai (focusing on the family jewels). Unable to work because of the attack's severity, Qiu goes to see Wang for an explanation. Wang is unrepentant, so Qiu goes to see a local policeman, who orders Wang to pay a 200 RMB fine and apologize. Wang reluctantly pays the cash but refuses to apologize. This indignity sets Qiu on a mission for justice. Still pregnant, she sets off to the provincial capital to make her case. The contrast between the poor Qiu and the more upscale city folk is great, but she struggles on and obtains a promise that police will come to the village to investigate further. The police arrive and take Qinglai to the hospital for an X-ray. In the meantime, Qiu goes into labor. It being the height of winter and with Qiu suffering complications, she must reluctantly accept Wang's assistance in getting to the hospital. Having saved Qiu and her baby's life, she is so grateful that she invites Wang to the child's "one month party". But the news is in: Qinglai suffered a broken rib in the attack and Wang was therefore sent to prison.

The way audiences react to the film is very telling of cultural differences: in China it was lauded as a triumphant comedy, while in the West it is received as a somber melodrama.

马路
天使

Malu Tianshi

Street Angel
1937

Zhou Xuan, the star of *Street Angel*, was only 19 years old when the film was made, but the legacy of the singer/ actress dubbed the "Golden Voice" lives on. She only made 20 or so films in the 1930s and '40s, but go to any Chinese flea market today and you'll find vintage pictures of the starlet. Her lowly beginnings – abandoned by her parents after she was born and nearly sold into prostitution by her foster parents as a teen – serve her well in the role of Xiao Hong, a teahouse singer who, along with her sister Xiao Yun and a ragtag bunch of urban youths, struggles to eke out a meager existence in the slums of Shanghai.

Having left northeast China for Shanghai, the two sisters find themselves at the mercy of the Shanghai landlords who act as their guardians. The younger Xiao Hong, is made to sing with her nightingale voice, but the older Xiao Yun (Zhao Huishen) is forced into prostitution. With her melancholic disposition, sultry, almost goth appearance, Xiao Yun haunts the picture and is, as most cinematic prostitutes in this time, a symbol of suffering in an unjust society. But their lives are not entirely bleak: Chen Xiaoping (Zhao Dan), a trumpet player in a marching band, falls madly in love with Xiao Hong. His knockabout group of friends provides much needed comic relief to this urban tragedy and they come to Xiao Hong's aid when her landlord promises to sell her to a local gangster as a concubine. They first attempt to prosecute the landlord, but find out the law is only the reserve of the rich, so they instead help Xiao Hong run away to another district of Shanghai. Xiao Yun also dreams of escaping and

Director
Yuan Muzhi

Screenwriter
Yuan Muzhi

Cast
Zhou Xuan
Zhao Huishen
Zhao Dan

Running time
87 minutes

182

starting a new life with Chen's friend Zhang, but when the gangster comes after the sisters Xiao Hong escapes but Xiao Yun is stabbed. The film ends with Xiao Yun dying on a bed surrounded by her friends. They call for a doctor, but he won't come if they can't afford to pay for his services.

Street Angel was actually inspired by a Hollywood film from 1928 of the same name. Starring Janet Gaynor and directed by Frank Borzage, it's a tale of an Italian girl who runs away to join the circus. The film, which adds many Chinese attributes to the original, has enjoyed much critical acclaim over the years. Some see it as a strong indication that Chinese films had by the '30s developed a unique technical style, a precursor to both Italian neo-realist films and the great Chinese talkies to come. Whichever way you cut it, it's the finest screen performance by a Chinese starlet whose life, like that of so many performers of her generation, would ultimately end in tragedy.

IN THE MOOD FOR LOVE

The Chinese title for Hong Kong director Wong Kar-wai's film In the Mood for Love is Huayang Nianhua, the name of one of Zhou Xuan's most popular songs from the 1940s. Zhou Xuan's influence on the film, both visually and aurally, is obvious and her music is featured throughout.

Zhixi

Suffocation
2005

As China entered the new millennium, horror – a genre which had been conspicuously absent from Chinese cinemas for almost 40 years – started to reemerge. Buoyed by the underground international success of Asian horror movies like Japan's *The Ring*, Chinese filmmakers began to explore the supernatural and violent themes that had been taboo for the strictly controlled state-run production companies of previous generations. Celebrating this newfound freedom is *Suffocation* – its promotional information trumpeted it as "China's first psycho movie" – a lurid and dreamlike effort closer to the films of Alfred Hitchcock than anything from Japan or South Korea.

Ge You, the unmistakable bald comedic actor, has often proved his depth in dramatic roles, but in *Suffocation* he was forced to stretch himself even further. His character, Shen Xiao, is a schizophrenic photographer haunted by the notion that he murdered his wife after she cuckolded him, but his psychological instability means he can't be certain if he actually did. Ge's performance creates a corridor of uncertainty between his dreams and waking moments, plagued with visions of his missing wife and her cello case – in which he hid the body. Or did he? In his debut film, director Zhang Bingjing uses a mix of different film stocks, jarring editing and camera trickery to disorient the viewer and build tension. Yet this is very much Ge's movie, whose skilled performance brings to life his character's internal struggle.

Suffocation is one of only a handful of Chinese movies in this genre, and unfortunately it appears that we might

Director
Zhang Bingjian

Screenwriter
Gu Xiaoni

Cast
Ge You
Li Bin
Qin Hailu

Running time
86 minutes

not get to see more for a while. In the run up to the Beijing
Olympics in 2006, the State Administration of Radio, Film
and Television (SARFT) announced that all films containing
"wronged spirits and violent ghosts, monsters, demons,
and other inhuman portrayals, strange and supernatural
storytelling for the sole purpose of seeking terror and
horror" will be banned so as to "control and cleanse the
negative effect these items have on society, and to prevent
horrific, violent, cruel publications from entering the market
through official channels and to protect adolescents'
psychological health". The implementation of this protocol
has been uneven at best. American, Japanese and South
Korean horror movies remain on the shelves at nearly
every DVD store and films like the *Harry Potter* franchise
seem to have no problem getting into Chinese cinemas
despite supernatural elements and monsters. But as far as
production goes, films like *Suffocation* are probably the last
in a very short-lived genre – for now.

Yihe Yuan

Summer Palace
2006

Towards the end of the 1980s, a group of passionate and open-minded university students ride the wave of reform that is sweeping through Beijing and the rest of China. They listen to jazz music, fall in and out of bed with each other, and, one evening in June, climb aboard the convoy of buses heading to the demonstrations in Tian'anmen Square. Lou Ye's opus may have made censors wince and prudes blush, but there exists no finer examination of the psyche of those involved in the buildup, confrontation and aftermath of the defining moment of late 20th century Chinese history.

Yu Hong (Hao Lei) is a rural student, who earns a place at the fictional Beiqing University. Yu befriends Li Ti, an impressionable girl who – like Yu and their countless dormmates – is in the midst of a seismic sexual awakening. Yu and the intense Zhou Wei (Guo Xiaodong) become locked in a tempestuous relationship filled with passion and anger, feelings palpably reflecting the attitudes of their fellow students. As the volatility of their partnership increases, so do on-campus tensions, leading to the first-half climax when sexual frustration, angst and repression ignite on that fateful night in June. The film then flashes forward 10 years and catches up with Zhou, Yu and their classmates, now scattered around the globe. In Shenzhen, Wuhan and Berlin, they find solace in self-imposed exile, yet their youthful idealism has been replaced by fully formed cynicism forged in the fires of the massacre. They are paralyzed by their memories: unable to confront the past, but incapable of moving on.

Director
Lou Ye

Screenwriters
Lou Ye
Feng Mei
Ma Yingli

Cast
Hao Lei
Guo Xiaodong
Bai Xueyun
Cui Lin

Running time
140 minutes

"Zhou Wei, I want to break up with you."
"Why?"
"Because I can't leave you."

Iranian pianist Peyman Yazdanian's score is somber yet compelling, almost ironically juxtaposed with flashes of cheesy American pop – the first example of Western culture seeping into the students' lives. Yu's diary is narrated to enhance the film's dramatic effect; his musings go beyond what is clearly visible on screen and venture into the emotional cauldron simmering away inside the protagonist.

Lou keeps the actual events of Tian'anmen at a distance, focusing instead on the thoughts and feelings of the confused group of students. The full-frontal nudity, which is relatively uncommon in Chinese cinema, adds to the film's brutally honest approach. The film was selected to compete at the Cannes Film Festival in 2006, but, as Lou Ye and his producers had not received permission from the State Administration for Radio, Film and Television (SARFT), they were all slapped with a five-year ban from filmmaking.

The Swordsman in Double-Flag Town
1991

Shuangqizhen Daoke

Director
He Ping

Screenwriters
Yang Zhengguang
He Ping

Cast
Gao Wei
Zhao Mana
Chang Jiang
Sun Haiying
Wang Gang

Running time
91 minutes

The Western is one of the oldest and most versatile genres in cinematic history. It is an unmistakably American invention, but has transcended national boundaries. Sergio Leone breathed life into the fading genre in the 1960s with his "Man With No Name" trilogy (called "spaghetti Westerns" despite being primarily shot in Spain). But the aesthetic has proved even more adaptable. As a filmmaker, He Ping specialized in documentary films and stage performances, but he was also the first director to see the startling geographical parallels between western China and the US. *The Swordsman in Double-Flag Town* takes place in the deserts of northwest China, using the barren and inhospitable landscape to dwarf the inhabitants of these towns in a manner similar to Leone and John Ford before him.

The plot of *Swordsman* has all the familiar trappings of the Western but the six-shooters and duels are replaced with swords and kung fu. Whereas Leone had Clint Eastwood, He has Gao Wei as the teenage swordsman Haige. At the behest of his father's dying wish, Haige arrives in Double-Flag Town to claim his young bride. Double-Flag Town is a dangerous place presided over by the "One-Strike Swordsman", a deadly combatant Haige witnesses killing two people as he arrives. He finds his supposed "bride", Haomei, and her crippled innkeeper father, but neither is pleased to see him. Although sympathetic enough to let him stay, the innkeeper refuses to let him marry Haomei despite the previous agreement. Haige later witnesses a drunken swordsman attempt to rape Haomei and valiantly intervenes. Despite looking

188

tremendously mismatched, Haige miraculously kills the swordsman. The fight scene – a montage of flashing blades and dripping blood – is reminiscent of the more brutal Japanese samurai pictures, but with a hint of Hong Kong action. The townspeople declare Haige a hero and elevate him to the role of protector. In the jubilation, Haomei's father relents and agrees to the union with Haige, but their bliss is put on hold when the One-Strike Swordsman returns to town to avenge his murdered would-be rapist brother.

The film's climax employs a rich mix of cinematic traditions. The long shots of the face off in the center of the town could be taken from any number of genre films, but He Ping's delicate restraint with speed and a mix of enclosed and open spaces in the cinematography make the ending as engrossing as any of the films it attempts to emulate. When Haige dispatches his foe and rides off into the sunset, we are left with a film that is not only a worthy addition to the Western canon, but also proves that by the 1990s, Mainland Chinese cinema was finally ready to make action films that could rival those coming out of Hong Kong.

Shisan Ke Paotong

Thirteen Princess Trees
2006

Lü Yue is one of China's elite cinematographers – working on films like Zhang Yimou's *To Live* and Jon Woo's *Red Cliff* – but with *Thirteen Princess Trees* he proved himself also a consummate director. His fourth directorial effort, adapted from a novel of the same name (dubbed the Chinese *Catcher in the Rye)*, stirred up both controversy and critical acclaim. Teenage angst is somewhat virgin territory in Chinese films (no pun intended), but *Thirteen Princess Trees* strikes the right balance, never condescending to its characters or flinching away from honest depictions of the realities facing China's youth. Swapping his typical highly stylized camera work for a more low-fi digital video look, Lü uses a cinematographic approach better suited to the screenplay, capturing his subjects without overpowering them.

The film, set in the fictional Thirteen Princess Trees High School in Chengdu, opens with a student who has taken a classmate hostage at knifepoint. The rest of the film is told through flashback. Central to the film, and the angst it tries to conveys, is Feng (Liu Xin), a teenage girl with tomboy sensibilities. Feng has an unhealthy obsession with knives and dates the popular Taotao (Duan Bown). When a bully, Bao (Zhao Mengqiao), arrives after being expelled from other schools, things get more complicated. Although the older Bao terrorizes most of the class, Feng is still attracted to him. The film bursts with awkward relationships: from the domineering and strangely aggressive relationship of Bao and Feng to the unrequited lesbian attraction of Feng's best friend, Jojo (Wang Jing). The tracksuit-clad students of this

Director
Lü Yue

Screenwriters
Liu Ying
Lü Yue
He Dacao (novel)

Cast
Liu Xin
Duan Bowen
Zhao Mengqiao
Chen Keliang
Wang Jing
Luo Yadan
Shang Hui

Running time
98 minutes

fictional Chengdu school are disillusioned and confused, and, for lack of healthy alternatives, things can often turn violent.

When making this film, Lü Yue spoke of wanting to make a film that connected with a younger audience, many of whom feel confined by society and their circumstances. His film also contains a powerful cautionary message of how the problems of today's youth breed armies of apathetic adults. It was never going to be easy for Lü Yue to bring this novel to the big screen in China and it received numerous snips at the hands of censors. The scenes removed involved a rape, suggestions of homosexuality, and a teacher's suicide, and without these hard-hitting moments, much of the film's dramatic resonance is lost. Outside of its correct cultural context, the film might appear naïve – just another movie about moody teenagers with arbitrary problems – but in China, where teenage issues get so little attention, it's groundbreaking.

Wo Zhe Yibeizi

This Life of Mine
1950

Made shortly after the forming of the People's Republic of China, *This Life of Mine* is a reasonably faithful adaptation of a novel by one of China's most important 20th century writers, Lao She. Shi Hui, who had become an established actor in the 1940s, directs and stars in this bittersweet story of a policeman in "old Beijing" society. A strong political message – which must have delighted the new Communist government – along with touching acting and iconic scenes of a Beijing that has since almost entirely disappeared, make this one of China's most enduring literary adaptations.

The story is presented in the first person, with Shi Hui playing the narrator, who endures terrible hardships from the tail end of the Qing Dynasty through the Republican era up to October 1, 1949 and the arrival of the Communists. As a young man with little education, the only career open to him is the police force, but his ability to settle petty disputes as he patrols the *hutongs* is not enough to help him stand up against the warlords that plague the city. After the Kuomintang come to power, he is assigned to guard a corrupt official, who soon becomes the target of dissatisfied students during the May Fourth Movement of 1919. The narrator befriends the leader of the movement, Shen Yuan, a student who foresees a better future for China's citizens. But with so much upheaval and so many broken promises from constantly changing governments, he refuses to think things will get any better. After his daughter is taken away by the Japanese, the narrator allows his son to join Shen Yuan and the other Communists outside of Beijing. With

Director
Shi Hui

Writer
Yang Liuqing

Cast
Shi Hui
Shen Yang
Cheng Zhi
Wei Heling
Li Wei
Cui Chaoming

Running time
108 minutes

"If there's a big problem, make it small; if there's a little problem, make it disappear."

little left to spur him on, the narrator passes away on the eve of the Communists return. The film ends on a somber yet optimistic note, showing the bright future that (they hoped) the PRC would bring.

It's amazing to see Beijing as it existed in those days: a city of tight-knit communities living in claustrophobic *hutongs*. Life was cheap and the political vacuum that came with the fall of the Qing Dynasty brought nothing but suffering to many, while corrupt officials lived in luxury; a discrepancy successfully attacked in the film.

For Shi Hui, creating such a flattering piece of political filmmaking should have guaranteed him a safe future under the Communists, but he was labeled a rightist during the Anti-Rightist Campaign of 1957 and publicly humiliated. Out of protest, Shi Hui took his own life, robbing future generations of one of China's finest actors.

Huozhe

To Live
1994

To live in China is to suffer, endure, but ultimately carry on. This is the stoic message of Zhang Yimou's portrait of a family living through China's tumultuous recent history. Ge You, recognizable mainly for his comic performances, is a dominant presence as an aristocratic gambler turned peasant, and Gong Li – starring in yet another of Zhang's films – excels again as his long-suffering wife. Together, they elicit sympathy with restrained performances amidst scenes that could easily devolve into melodrama with weaker actors.

As with Chen Kaige's *Farewell My Concubine*, Zhang Yimou adapts a novel (*To Live* by Yu Hua) to tell an emotive story about people trying to survive in Mao-era China. The film opens on the charismatic Xu Fugui (Ge Lou), a gambler who fritters away his ancestral home in a series of dice games. Fed up with his outrageous behavior, his wife Jiazhen (Gong Li) takes his two children and leaves. Fugui eventually wins them back, but not before taking a lowly job as a shadow puppeteer in the town drinking den. This reconciliation is short lived, and before long, he is swept up with the Nationalist army in the Chinese Civil War. Managing to switch sides to the People's Liberation Army and return home, Fugui and his family begin to live and work communally as part of Mao's Great Leap Forward. Tragedy strikes at every turn. Fugui and Jiazhen lose their son to a car accident and countless friends to political turmoil. Managing to stay below the radar and avoid direct criticism or violence, the couple emerges from the Cultural Revolution alive but jaded and broken.

Director
Zhang Yimou

Screenwriters
Lu Wei
Yu Hua (novel)

Cinematographer
Lü Yue

Cast
Ge You
Gong Li
Niu Ben
Guo Tao
Jiang Wu

Running time
125 minutes

"Little bastards from big bastards grow. I learned all I know from you."

For Zhang Yimou and his peers at the 1980s Beijing Film Academy, the Cultural Revolution provided the richest source material. He described *To Live* as his most personal film, based as it was on a period where all terrible facets of human nature were exposed. When the film was released in 1994, Chinese filmmakers had received a directive banning them from featuring any scenes from that era in their movies. Regardless of these instructions, Zhang Yimou realized the importance of keeping these stories of hardship alive in order to heal the wounds from this period. As gripping and tearful as you could imagine, his film is a brilliant blend of consummate acting and subtle but beautiful direction.

ELECTRIC SHADOWS

When moving images were first screened in China in 1896, a film was called an "electric shadow play" (dianguang yingxi) or simply "electric shadow" (dianying) because no equivalent existed in the Chinese lexicon for "film". The term is derived from the shadow puppet plays that were popular in China at the time. In To Live, Ge You's character puts on shows using the original shadow puppets to entertain gamblers at drinking dens and the People's Liberation Army.

Wan Zhu

The Trouble-shooters
1989

It's disappointing that China's first decade back out in the open was also one that style forgot: the 1980s. So as China was just coming to grips with newfound freedoms and cultural expressions, their films were riddled with cheesy music, appalling fashion sense and mullets. Not that *The Trouble-shooters*, as it may appear at first glance, is purely a comedic exercise. Beneath its surface bubbles a strong social critique and political message brought to the fore by writer Wang Shuo – one of the most important novelists of the period. Coinciding with a number of other "incidents" occurring in Beijing in 1989, the film is notable for accurately portraying the restlessness and angst about to boil over.

Three unemployed young men club together to form a company called 3T. Their organization will do those things nobody wants to do – like step in on a blind date – for a price. Their biggest challenge comes when they have to stage an awards ceremony to make a mediocre writer feel better about himself. The trio conjures up a bizarre fusion of burlesque, music hall and fashion show, with aspects of China's past and present colliding: Peking Opera performers struggle with female body builders for elbow space on the runway. Unluckily for 3T, no other authors show up for the award, so their friends must impersonate them. These unlikely capitalist endeavors soon land 3T in trouble. When the group is assigned to look after an old lady whose children won't visit her in the hospital, they are blamed when she commits suicide. A lawsuit filed by the disgruntled author further compounds their worries. What started out

Director
Mi Jiashan

Screenwriters
Wang Shuo
Mi Jiashan

Cast
Zhang Guoli
Liang Tian
Li Geng
Ge You
Ma Xiaoqing
Pan Hong

Running time
101 minutes

"The foreigners are coming here to taste Chinese food. Can't you see their bellies?"

as a clever way to earn money brings the group much heartache.

The Trouble-shooters is most notable for the early appearance of Ge You, a man who would go on to become the premier comedic actor of his generation. The famously bald performer here clings to his last follicles as the hapless Yu and, even at this early stage in his career, flashes of his brilliance can be seen. The film is at its most cutting in its illustrations of public figures amidst scenes of chaos, such as when a traffic cop frantically gestures to the cars around him but no one pays him any attention. Wang Shuo became this generation's voice of urban China and, although his work in this film may appear somewhat simplistic and farcical, his portrait of a transitioning society in disarray struck a chord with young audiences.

Tuya de Hunshi

Tuya's Marriage
2006

Tuya's Marriage is a film set in the geographical fringes of China, where grasslands of Inner Mongolia are slowly turning to desert, and its people's nomadic way of life is threatened. It's often easy to forget that China is a hugely diverse country, both in terms of environment and ethnicity. In some ways, mostly aesthetic, the film feels like a Western, but *Tuya's Marriage* is a uniquely Chinese affair that strives to show how even the lives of those furthest away from China's industrial centers feel the effects of modernization.

Tuya, played by director Wang Quanan's frequent collaborator Yu Nan, is a modern-day frontierswoman. Her husband was disabled in a drilling accident, so she must single-handedly raise two children and herd their sheep, but she never complains. Seeing her health diminish, Tuya's husband suggests that she divorce him and find a new husband who can help support her. Reluctant at first, Tuya finally relents. From their foolish neighbor, Shenghe, whose own wife keeps deserting him, to a rich oil baron, Tuya's beauty attracts a wave of suitors to their yurt's entrance. Her one stipulation is that they must also take care of her original husband, something that most, in order to save face, are unwilling to do. Tuya is caught between two worlds, as her traditions conflict with her pragmatism in a situation that requires the latter. If she can't raise her sheep, with only a camel and horse to help her, her family will starve.

Such a bleak story (and environment) does not mean *Tuya's Marriage* is without sensitivity or humor. The neighbor, Shenghe, is a well-meaning idiot who tries again and again

Director
Wang Quanan

Screenwriters
Wang Quanan
Lu Wei

Cast
Yu Nan

Running time
86 minutes

"Don't be afraid, if wolves were coming Mama would eat them."

to finish digging the well that Tuya's husband had started. The parade of gormless men seeking Tuya's hand is also good for a few laughs. Using many untrained actors, the film is more a drama than an ethnography of Inner Mongolia and it came under attack for having the characters speak Mandarin rather than the native Mongolian dialect. In most other aspects, however, it is faithful to the lifestyles and customs of the nomadic people it depicts.

The film appeared at a time when Chinese films were gaining traction at international film festivals and *Tuya's Marriage* scooped up the top prize of the Golden Bear at the Berlin International Film Festival. This prestigious award was won in no small part thanks to the performance of Yu Nan. This woman from Dalian (northeast China) transforms herself into the part of a woman that seems to be carrying the entire world on her shoulders, and the performance adds emotional depth to an already beautifully shot film about a lesser-known Chinese region.

Wutai Jiemei

Two Stage Sisters
1965

Two Stage Sisters was director Xie Jin's last film before the Cultural Revolution. Strange for a work so rich in communist rhetoric, it was savagely attacked for its "bourgeois" sensibilities and not released to the general public until after 1976.

Chunhua is a young widow on the run from her in-laws, who want to sell her into another marriage. She happens upon a Shaoxing opera troupe's performance and begs them to take her with them. They agree and she becomes fast friends with Yuehong – the actress who plays the male roles in the all-female opera company. After Yuehong's father dies, the troupe is disbanded, and the two friends are sold to a Shanghai-based theater group, where they will replace a fading star. In contrast to the glamour of the stage, everyday life is tough: they work long hours and are virtually penniless. Tang, the cruel stage manager, is a constant annoyance, but Yuehong eventually falls in love with him. Soon after the romance begins, the sisters' relationship is strained and they eventually separate. Chunhua continues on with her career and is inspired by a radical female journalist, imbuing her performances with a political flavor. Seeking to silence Chunhua, Tang has her tried as a radical and persuades Yuehong to testify. The prosecution does not stand up in court and Yuehong, publicly humiliated, flees to the countryside. Tang fears a backlash from the Communist Party, soon to take power, and flees to Taiwan with the Nationalist government. The film ends on an upbeat note. Chunhua tracks down

Director
Xie Jin

Screenwriters
Wang Lingu
Xu Jin
Xie Jin

Cast
Cao Yindi
Xie Fang
Gao Yuansheng
Shangguan Yunzhu
Li Wei

Running time
108 minutes

"Our fate is not great, we are only actresses."

Yuehong after the Communists liberate Shanghai and they mend their relationship.

In his time and context, Xie Jin was peerless. His directorial skill and agility with the camera were something at which to marvel. He absorbed the techniques of Hollywood, but used them to create stories that rang true with the Chinese people. His focus on strong female characters, as in *Woman Basketball Player No. 5* and *The Red Detachment of Women*, was a signal of a director comfortable working outside the established norms. It's a pity that his career was stopped in its tracks by the Cultural Revolution. We can only imagine what he might have been able to achieve during those lost years.

Baimao Nü

The White-Haired Girl
1950

Directors
Wang Bin
Shui Hua

Screenwriters
Wang Bin
Shui Hua
Yang Runshen

Cast
Tian Hua
Chen Qiang
Li Baiwan
Hu Peng

Running time
106 minutes

It took until January of 1952 for the last of the Chinese film studios to be nationalized, but, just a year after the Communists came to power in 1949, the films being produced in China were dripping with admiration for the new regime. *The White-Haired Girl* was always going to be a red-hot communist fable. The opera upon which it was based was conceived in Yan'an – the Communist stronghold from which Mao Zedong led his war of resistance against the Japanese. The story was derived from a combination of local Shaanxi legends about peasants being abused and mistreated until they went insane. These accounts, combined with a legend about an immortal woman with white hair, inspired one of China's defining class conflict dramas, which retains much of its vigor to this day.

Qian Jiang's cinematography is littered with craggy mountains, foreboding and menacing, but it's not until late in the film that their impact is felt. At the start, everything is rosy. Yang Bailao (Zhang Shouwei) is a tenant farmer who lives a life of peaceful contentment with his daughter Xi'er (Tian Hua). Xi'er is in love with her neighbor, Dachun, and the couple is due to be married after the harvest is complete. But for this pair, happiness is a commodity with a short shelf-life. Chen Qiang, who plays the diabolical landlord Huang Shiren, is epically villainous, so believable in this role that he was harassed in the street by those unwilling (or unable) to separate fact and fiction. Yang is massively in debt to Huang and is pressured into signing his daughter over to work in servitude for Huang. Overcome with shame, Yang takes his

"You say I'm a ghost? You made me like this!"

life and the landlord capitalizes on the vulnerability of Xi'er, raping her and chasing Dachun out of the village. With the help of a friendly maid, Xi'er escapes the clutches of Huang and runs away, deep into the mountains. Through stress and despair her hair turns completely white and she begins to live a pitiful existence as a hermit, occasionally stealing offerings from temples. The appearances of a ghostly white figure are interpreted as a spiritual apparition among the villagers. Meanwhile, Dachun heads off in search of the Red Army to help him liberate the village. He returns two years later to mobilize the villagers and, on hearing the tales of a white-haired woman living in the caves, he seeks and is reunited with his lover. Justice is served, but only when Huang is executed for his crimes.

Wish fulfillment? Perhaps for many, but overcoming adversity is a universal theme and, in this sense, the Communist films of this period connected with most audiences, who were more than happy to see the old evil landlord get his comeuppance.

Nülan Wuhao

Woman Basketball Player No. 5
1957

Woman Basketball Player No. 5 was a quiet explosion in Chinese cinema. The first sports film in color, it gripped audiences with a vitality and speed unlike any other Chinese film that came before. It was also the breakthrough film of director Xie Jin, who remained active throughout some of Chinese cinemas most difficult periods right up to his death in 2008. Xie was relatively inexperienced here, but his film gushes with the conventions that would become staples of the sports movie genre: training montages, flashbacks and truly impressive (for the time) sports scenes.

Tian Zhenhua is the stoic, if somewhat weathered, newly appointed basketball coach of Shanghai's female basketball team. Years before, he had been the star basketball player in Shanghai, where he fell in love with the coach's daughter, Lin Jie. During an important game against some foreign (and especially big-nosed) marines, the coach took a bribe and told the team to throw the match. But pride overwhelmed Tian. He battled on to win the game, but was beaten up afterwards and Jie's father forced her to marry someone else. Flash-forward to Tian's coaching days. He has become intrigued by one particular player: No. 5, Lin Xiaojie. She's a great player and, as luck would have it, the daughter of Tian's lost love. Fate and basketball align to remove Lin's husband from the picture and bring the old couple back together.

Cheesy, perhaps, and boasting a spectacularly clumsy English title, but *Woman Basketball Player No. 5* is still a star in the sports genre. Jin illustrates China's generational divide beautifully, as the virtuous and unemotional elders

Director
Xie Jin

Screenwriter
Xie Jin

Cast
Liu Qiong
Yu Mingde
Qin Yi
Cui Chaoming
Xiang Mei

Studio
Tianma Films

Running time
86 minutes

"I will never forget that game. We played so well in the first half, but then the boss sold us out."

clash with the teenage girls, who can switch from giggly coquettishness to steely determination in the blink of an eyelash. The color scheme in the film is also beautiful, with the tricolor film stock turning reds, greens and blues into bright, dominating forces on the screen. The political undertones of the film are relevant, but refreshingly take a back seat to plot and direction giving *Woman Basketball Player No. 5* the feel of a complete article, rather than the hastily assembled parts of Western techniques and Chinese political philosophy. Oh, and it's also the film that made basketball in China cool, long before Yao Ming put on a Houston Rockets jersey.

Xiang Hun Nü

Woman Sesame-Oil Maker
1993

If we look at the general characterization of women in Chinese films over the last 30 years, certain patterns emerge: the female has a will of iron and the moral fortitude to endure even the most unspeakable suffering. Siqin Gaowa is an actress whose trademark is playing such women. In *The Call of the Front* (1979), she rose to prominence as a peasant girl who falls in love with the wounded soldier she nurses and in *Rickshaw Boy* she played a bad-tempered spinster. In *Woman Sesame-Oil Maker* – despite its clunky English name – she best exemplifies the hardships of many women in contemporary Chinese society with a restrained but powerful performance.

Xiang (Siqin Gaowa) is an illiterate peasant with little say in her destiny, having been betrothed when she was just a child. Despite these hindrances, she has a gift for making sesame oil and her diligence has made her the richest person in her village. Her family life is not as rosy. Her husband is an abusive drunk and her mentally disabled son, Dunzi, suffers from frequent epileptic fits. Some good (financial) fortune comes Xiang's way when a Japanese woman is impressed by the quality of her sesame mill and decides to become an investor. Selflessly, Xiang decides to use the money as a dowry to give her son a chance at marrying. Dunzi has long been infatuated with a girl, Huanhuan, and because of her family's dire financial circumstances she is forced to marry him. After being humiliated on her wedding day by her new husband, Huanhuan is reassured by Xiang, who relates details of her own unhappy marriage. The union is not easy

Director
Xie Fei

Screenwriter
Xie Fei

Cast
Siqin Gaowa
Wu Yujuan
Lei Luosheng
Chen Baoguo

Running time
105 minutes

for Huanhuan, especially when Dunzi nearly strangles her during one of his fits. She attempts to go back to her family but they won't allow it.

Huanhuan later witnesses Xiang being violently beaten by her drunken husband. Xiang takes a lover, but her husband comes home unexpectedly and the man has to escape through the window, where he is witnessed by Huanhuan. The lover breaks off the affair, and Huanhuan keeps the secret. The two bitterly unhappy women form an unspoken, almost psychic bond. When Xiang sees teeth marks on Huanhuan's skin – obviously caused by her own son – and understands the misery she has caused, she implores Huanhuan to get a divorce. But the film ends on a bleak note: Huanhuan decides to continue on because, as she sees it, her life is already ruined.

Tianxia Wu Zei

A World Without Thieves
2004

Feng Xiaogang's films are the bread and butter of Chinese cinema. Often comedies, they use down-to-earth language and humor and are usually released around Chinese New Year, when people return home to be with their families. Oh, and his films make lots and lots of money. But their commercial appeal is no reason to dismiss them, like many critics, as populist trash. *A World Without Thieves*, unlike Feng's other *hesui pian* (New Year's films), ends on a rather tragic note. The film still contains sufficient levels of comedy, though, and with Hong Kong superstar Andy Lau cast in the leading role it was a surefire hit.

Wang Bo (Lau) and Wang Li (Rene Liu) are a pair of thieves, who have just traveled to Tibet to sell a car that they acquired by blackmailing a womanizing businessman. On the train back inland, they encounter Sha Gen (Wang Baoqiang), who is the definition of innocence. The boy has saved up 60,000 RMB over five years to pay for his marriage. Rather than having the money wired, he would rather carry the money himself during the 48-hour train journey, believing that he lives in a world without thieves. Wang Bo believes that stealing the cash would help them start a new life, while Wang Li (who recently discovered she is pregnant with Wang Bo's child) wants to protect the naive Sha Gen. Things are further complicated when Hu Li (regular Feng collaborator Ge You playing against type) and his dastardly band of thieves board the train. The two sides battle over the cash while the train races towards Beijing. Alas, the "happy" ending comes at a great price for Wang Bo and Wang Lu.

Director
Feng Xiaogang

Screenwriters
Feng Xiaogang
Wang Gang
Lin Lisheng
Zhang Jialu

Cast
Andy Lau
Rene Liu
Ge You
Li Bingbing

Running time
113 minutes

208

"In the 21st-century, what's the most valuable thing? Talent!"

From a principally visual point of view, the hyper-stylized film excels when depicting its kung fu-like brand of pick-pocketing inside the train, and the breathtaking Tibetan plains oustide. Pretty boy Andy Lau, despite sporting a ridiculous haircut, does well as the genuinely conflicted Wang Bo, who grapples with the idea that once a thief, always a thief. All the while, the visions of Tibet, with its Buddhist spiritual heritage, beg the question of whether there is a better alternative to the thieves' hyper-materialistic lifestyle.

Huang Tudi

Yellow Earth
1984

The gestation period for the Fifth Generation of Chinese filmmakers was long and arduous. They had emerged, as the rest of the nation did, from 10 years of repression, malnourishment and general cultural anemia. The Cultural Revolution had robbed China of many of its finest artistic voices, but the new generation, who entered into the Beijing Film Academy when it reopened in 1978, was determined to produce works unlike anything that had come before it. Director Chen Kaige – a man who had been forced to denounce his own filmmaker father during the Cultural Revolution – along with cinematography graduate Zhang Yimou, broke from the boring, outmoded roles they had been assigned by Beijing Studio and went to work with Guangxi Studio on a film based upon the short story *Echoes in the Deep Valley*. The plot was simple: it's 1939 and a Communist soldier from Yan'an scours the neighboring countryside to collect folk songs from local farmers. Rather than reconstructing the script to suit their needs, Chen and Zhang decided, in bold avant-garde fashion, to tell the story almost entirely through visuals, using the bleak desolate land as the film's central figure.

Gu Qing (Wang Xueqi), the soldier searching for traditional songs to adapt into Communist propaganda tunes, meets a peasant family: father, daughter Cuiqiao (Bai Xue) and mute son Hanhan. The modern soldier is at odds with his backward hosts, but teaches them new ideas and, in return, they teach him their traditional values. Cuiqiao, eyes opened, questions her forthcoming arranged marriage,

Director
Chen Kaige

Screenwriters
Chen Kaige
Zhang Ziliang

Cinematographer
Zhang Yimou

Cast
Xue Bai
Wang Xueqi
Tan Tuo

Running time
89 minutes

seeing in Gu Qing and the Red Army a way to escape her petty existence. When Gu Qing departs with the promise of returning for Cuiqiao, she is forced to marry. Determined to leave, she sets off across the Yellow River, but drowns. The film closes ambiguously with a blend of montage and dissolving images of the villagers performing a ritualistic rain dance and shots of the bright blue sky contrasted with the barren yellow earth.

For Chen, the interaction of land, heaven and man is important, an idea taken from Daoist cosmology: man cannot succeed unless he is in harmony with the earth. The yellow countryside where the peasants live is beautiful, but barren. They are unable to support themselves from the land, which literally dwarfs them in Zhang's spectacular shots. *The Yellow Earth* presented a harsh critique of traditional Chinese culture, and also questioned the Communist Party's ability to actually save the poor. It is worthy of its reputation as the first great modern Chinese movie.

THE FIFTH GENERATION
The Fifth Generation refers to 1984 graduates of the Beijing Film Academy in 1984. They were the first filmmakers in the post-Mao era, and their films rejected the conventions that had previously characterized Chinese cinema. Working for small, rural film companies, directors like Chen Kaige, Zhang Yimou and Zhang Junzhao were at the forefront of a new cinematic movement, which spoke to a generation grappling with the horrific events of the previous decade.

Women Lia

You and Me
2005

Beijing's rapidly disappearing *hutong* alleyways are a link with the past. Elegantly narrow to the point of being claustrophobic, they are places where families and their neighbors live in each other's faces. When director Ma Liwen – actress-turned-protégé of Tian Zhuangzhuang – was a young student moving from her hometown in Jiangxi Province to Beijing, she, like a lot of people moving to the city, decided to rent a room in a small courtyard home (*siheyuan*) off of a hutong. As Ma undertook her studies at Central Academy of Drama, she was initially infuriated with the old female landlord with whom she shared a courtyard, but over time the generational clash lessened and they began to appreciate each other. It was this relationship that formed the kernel of *You and Me*, her first international hit.

First-time actress Gong Zhe was plucked from the obscurity of a university canteen to play the role of the recent-arrival Xiao Ma. Beijing is bitterly cold and she likes the location and tranquility of a dilapidated home, so Xiao Ma decides to pay the inflated price given by an old battle-axe of a widow, Grandma (Jia Yaqin). Things start off poorly for Xiao Ma and her penny-pinching landlord – Grandma refuses to allow her to install a telephone and demands a cut from the money Ma raises clearing out junk in the courtyard. After periods of intense squabbling, Grandma becomes inquisitive about Xiao Ma's love life and even suggests her grandson as a potential match. Despite being a little put off by the suggestion, the gesture opens a door to warmer feelings between the pair. The subtle way in which

Director
Ma Liwen

Screenwriter
Ma Liwen

Cast
Jin Yaqin
Gong Zhe

Running time
83 minutes

the gradual thaw unfolds is the greatest achievement of the film. The affection the characters show as they begin to understand each other is truly remarkable, and nothing feels forced in this film as it slowly unfolds over four Beijing seasons.

Drawing from her stage background, Ma sets the action almost entirely within the walls of the courtyard, and proves her directorial skill in creating the tension necessary to balance out a rather simple plot. The film draws you in, forcing you to engage and empathize with the characters, and closes on a somber note that can't fail to touch its audience.

Image Credits

Cover, *Early Spring in February* courtesy of China Film Association
Back cover, *Song at Midnight* courtesy of China Film Association
Page 3, *The Founding of a Republic* courtesy of China Film Group
Page 4, *Sons and Daughters of the Grassland* courtesy of China Film Association
Page 5, *Havoc in Heaven* courtesy of China Film Association
Page 6, *Still Life* courtesy of Xstream Pictures
Page 8, *The Swordsman in Double-Flag Town* courtesy of Xi'an Film Studio
Page 9, *The Goddess* courtesy of China Film Association
Page 11, *Forever Enthralled* courtesy of China Film Group
Page 17, *The Assembly* courtesy of China Film Association
Page 19, *At the Middle Age* courtesy of China Film Association
Page 21, *Back to Back, Face to Face* courtesy of Xi'an Film Studio
Page 23, *Balzac and the Little Chinese Seamstress* courtesy of China Film Association
Page 25, *The Banquet* courtesy of China Film Association
Page 27, *Beijing Bicycle* courtesy of China Film Association
Page 29, *The Big Road* courtesy of China Film Association
Page 31, *Big Shot's Funeral* courtesy of Movie Art China
Page 33, *The Black Cannon Incident* courtesy of China Film Association
Page 35, *Black Snow* courtesy of Xi'an Film Studio
Page 37, *Blind Mountain* courtesy of the director
Page 39, *Blind Shaft* courtesy of the director
Page 41, *Blood on Wolf Mountain* courtesy of China Film Association
Page 43, *The Blue Kite* courtesy of China Film Association
Page 49, *Cheng the Fruit Seller* courtesy of China Film Association
Page 53, *Crazy Stone* courtesy of China Film Association
Page 55, *Crossroads* courtesy of China Film Association
Page 67, *Crows and Sparrows* courtesy of China Film Association
Page 59, *Devils on the Doorstep* courtesy of China Film Association
Page 61, *Early Spring in February* courtesy of China Film Association
Page 63, *East Palace, West Palace* courtesy of China Film Association
Page 65, *Eight Thousand Li of Cloud and Moon* courtesy of China Film Association
Page 67, *Farewell My Concubine* courtesy of Beijing Film Studio
Page 69, *Five Golden Flowers* courtesy of China Film Association
Page 71, *Forever Enthralled* courtesy of China Film Group
Page 73, *For Fun* courtesy of Beijing Film Studio
Page 75, *The Founding of a Republic* courtesy of China Film Group
Page 77, *Frozen* courtesy of China Film Association
Page 79, *Girl from Hunan* courtesy of Beijing Film College Youth Studio
Page 81, *The Goddess* courtesy of China Film Association
Page 85, *Good Morning, Beijing* courtesy of Beijing Film College Youth Studio
Page 87, *Havoc in Heaven* courtesy of China Film Association
Page 89, *Hero* courtesy of China Film Association
Page 91, *Hibiscus Town* courtesy of China Film Association
Page 93, *The Horse Thief* courtesy of China Film Association
Page 95, *House of Flying Daggers* courtesy of China Film Association
Page 97, *In The Heat of the Sun* courtesy of Movie Art China

Index

Movies by Release Year

Movies by Chinese Name

People